# Ethics for Everyone

## How to Increase Your Moral Intelligence

ARTHUR DOBRIN

John Wiley & Sons, Inc.

Published by John Wiley & Sons, Inc., New York
Published simultaneously in Canada

This publication is designed to provide accurate and authoritative information in regard to the subject matter covered. It is sold with the understanding that the publisher is not engaged in rendering professional services. If professional advice or other expert assistance is required, the services of a competent professional person should be sought.

*Library of Congress Cataloging-in-Publication Data*
Dobrin, Arthur, date.
    Ethics for everyone : how to increase your moral intelligence / Arthur Dobrin.
    p. cm.
    Includes bibliographical references and index.
    ISBN 0-471-43595-3(pbk.)
    1. Moral development.    I. Title.
BF723.M54 D625 2002
155.2'5—dc21                                                    2001046857

Printed in the United States of America

10 9 8 7 6 5 4 3 2 1

This discussion is not about any chance question, but about the way one should live.

PLATO, *The Republic*

# Contents

# Introduction

## *How to Use This Book*

This book is designed to help you improve your moral IQ in much the same way that a law student learns to become a lawyer. First there is a little theory about the nature of morality, next there is a quiz to provide you with a picture of how you think about ethical problems, and finally there are case studies of ethical problems.

Take the time to read Part One, "Ethics Matters." While you don't need to be a philosopher to make sound moral judgments, it does help to understand something about the ethics itself.

Next, take the ethical quiz in Part Two. Here you will find four moral problems. Read the instructions, then answer the questions. Keep a copy of your responses.

Then read the twenty-one case studies in Parts Three and Four. Each vignette is followed by a series of questions. Think about them carefully. Jot down your answers before reading my and another expert's comments. After you've read our responses to the problem, see how your answers compare with what you've read.

Finally, go back to the quiz in Part Two. Without referring to your previous responses, answer the questions to the four stories once more. Now look at your two sets of answers. Did you change your mind about anything? If you did, what was different? Why do you think your answers differed?

This kind of reflection, self-questioning, and comparison will help sharpen your ability to detect ethical issues and help improve your moral IQ by making you more sensitive to moral matters.

PART ONE

# Ethics Matters

I

∝ℰ☙

# Everyday Ethics

## Talking Ethics

One day, Irma made a call from a public phone booth. When she put down the receiver, quarters poured out of the coin return. Irma related this little drama to me one evening, then asked, "What should I do with the money?" She was serious. She really wanted to know. Keeping the money bothered her, she said, but she wasn't convinced that returning it was right, either. So Irma and I spent some time talking about it. The more we conversed, the deeper we went into the moral issues that were revealed. While the amount of money was small, the ethical issues that it raised were significant.

As the leader of the Ethical Humanist Society for more than thirty years, I have had people like Irma seek me out to talk about their moral quandaries. For many years I've led a discussion group called "Everyday Ethics," where people come to discuss ethical problems they face. Some of the problems are as small as Irma's, but others have been as significant as what to do about a relative who needs living assistance but refuses all help.

Most of the problems we talk about have to do with telling the truth, loyalty, and fairness, and they often involve matters of

money, work, relatives, and friends. They present conflicts of values and interests. We seldom start our discussions agreeing about
what the right thing to do is, and it isn't unusual for us to end in
disagreement. Somewhere along the line, though, each of us has
gained a better insight into the nature of morality. The dialogue
has served its purpose.

I think about these practical, common ethical issues on a daily
basis. This is what I do for a living. I am involved with people who
want to live an ethical life. They are concerned with how to live
responsibly. They want to know what it means to be moral and
how to go about achieving this. They are troubled by the conflicts they sometimes experience between personal happiness and
social responsibility; they often have difficulties weighing the
options for action when no course seems right. There is fuzziness
about personal likes and dislikes and some objective measure by
which to decide whether something is ethical. There is uncertainty about the relationship between practical outcomes and
principled positions. So people seek me out. They want to know
what I think. They want me to help them to think more clearly.
They want to check out their own feelings, to see if they are leading them down a moral path.

Members in the Ethical Movement have looked to me for
moral guidance. They're not looking to talk to a philosopher in
the academic sense. I'm not a technical ethicist. They seek me out
the way someone with spiritual questions goes to a clergyman,
not a theologian. They want someone who helps in a practical
way, not in an academic fashion.

## Living with Ethics

I have lived trying to puzzle out what it means to live a good life
in the real world. I've spent most of my life working with ordi-

nary people who are trying to cope as best they can in a world that rarely stresses ethics. Success is often a higher value; ambition is frequently more valued than caring is. And caring for oneself seems to be far more important than caring for the community. This isn't to say that success, ambition, and self-care aren't important. They are. But for us to live a good life, we must place them in a larger ethical setting. I've learned this over and over again from experience. The people who are happiest are mainly those who have learned how to balance their ethical values with other values.

In addition to my activities in the Ethical Movement, I am a professor of humanities at Hofstra University. There I teach literature, religious ethics, and the psychology of morality. This provides me with the opportunity to pursue ethical knowledge on a more theoretical level. I keep up with the latest studies. I keep abreast of the experiments and surveys that look at the way children grow up to be ethical adults. But even here, ethical problems arise. What do I do with a student who needs to get at least a C+ in my class because he would otherwise lose his scholarship but who doesn't deserve the grade? Do I keep strictly to my absence policy when a student really has been sick? In a seminar where everyone is required to contribute, how do I treat a student who is silent because she is afraid to speak up in public?

For a number of years I have been involved with bioethical questions. I was a member of the Human Subjects Review Board at a major teaching hospital for several years. This group made such decisions as whether a doctor could perform a needed procedure or offer an experimental drug. We looked to make sure that the patient understood what was being proposed and had not been unduly pressured to give his consent. We also had to weigh benefits against risks. Twice we rejected proposals because we thought that the means the researcher wanted to use weren't justified, even though the possible benefits for patients were great.

I am now a member of the Ethics Committee at Winthrop University Hospital, a teaching hospital in Mineola, New York. This group helps set policies for the hospital involving matters of life and death. One major discussion we had was about whether requests for permission to perform autopsies should be routine. On the one hand, we knew that interns need to practice on human bodies in order to learn their skills properly. On the other hand, it seemed cruel to ask a family's permission to do an autopsy on a loved one who has just died. The committee also struggled for more than a year to develop a policy about practicing medical procedures on the newly dead. Physicians in training use these bodies to learn how to insert venous catheters. But good medical ethical practice requires patient consent, something impossible to obtain under these circumstances.

Over the years I've also worked with many organizations dedicated to issues of social justice. One time I was at a meeting with the county police department about civilian charges of police abuse. The problem was how to make it possible for people to complain without feeling that they would face reprisals while also protecting police officers from having their careers ruined by charges that had no foundation. Another time I was on a committee concerned with financially troubled private hospitals that were being absorbed by a hospital that was based upon religious principles. The issue was how to provide medical services while not imposing religious rules upon all who came for care.

## Applying Ethics

This book is a result of my three decades of experience in grappling with both personal and social ethics. I've written it because you are probably much like the people I meet. You want to better understand what ethics is and what morality may demand of you. You want to be better able to deal with moral issues that confront you day after day at home, in your neighborhood, with your friends, or at work. In a sense, this is a textbook in applied ethics, but I've tried to stay clear of jargon and theory. The problems I present are different from those typically found in college texts, which are mainly centered on theory and concepts. This work is also different from ethics books written for particular professions—business, journalism, medicine, social work, and so forth. Those discuss mainly matters of law and social policy, with a focus on legislation or codes of ethics. Such books typically give scant attention to the kinds of ethical problems you are likely to face.

This book takes a different approach. It is written for anyone who is interested in ethics for its own sake. It is a book of people's ethics. It is for the kind of person who might seek my ethical counsel—someone interested in leading a good life.

The focus here is upon personal responsibility, not social policy, although sometimes it isn't possible to completely separate the two.

The examples of ethical problems I give are from real situations. A few of them are variations of problems that I have had to deal with myself. And a few are taken from my own life.

I want to provide you with a sense of what ethics is and how to better incorporate ethics and values into your daily life. You may well have found yourself in situations like the ones I present, and you may have wondered if you did the right thing. Each of the case studies in this book illustrates an issue of moral consideration. I give you my own responses to each of the problems, but I am not giving you *the* right answer. I want you to think along with me. That's the reason I have asked experts in a variety of fields to give their thoughts as well. You will find the comments of a parish priest and an African theologian, a psychotherapist and a philosopher, a scholar of Chinese ethics and an athlete, a businesswoman and a journalist, a social critic and a professional soldier, a medical researcher and a social worker, and many others.

While steering away from theory, I've also tried to avoid a how-to approach to ethics in which all the answers are prepacked and morality is a matter of learning the right lessons. The book doesn't give the "correct" answer to any moral problem. Rather, it presents a way to think about ethics. It is designed to help you think things through for yourself. If this book is successful, you will not necessarily be more sure that you have the right moral answer, but you will be sure that whatever answer you do arrive at will be built on a better foundation than before.

Let me add something here: I am not saying that a better understanding of ethics will necessarily make you a better person. Other things beside good judgment are needed for that. First, you have to want to be a better person. A person may know what the right thing is but choose not to do it. This is the way I feel about chess. I know the rules of the game, but I simply don't care to spend my time playing.

Second, you may want to be a better person, you may make sound judgments about living ethically, but you may feel that you can't do anything about a given situation. You may be afraid of what it will cost you, you may be afraid of what other people will say, or you may be afraid of becoming an outsider. You may not have the courage to do the right thing. You may not have the physical strength, or you may lack some other attribute. These are important considerations, and you can see why it is impossible to completely separate ethics from psychology.

So this book doesn't pretend to make you into an ethical person, but it does offer the possibility of raising your moral IQ, since its primary focus is on learning how to make ethical judgments.

This book is a kind of map, but an unusual one. The following fable, told by Rabbi Shmuel Avidor Hacohen, expresses the spirit in which I hope this book will be taken.

One day a hiker lost his way in the woods. No matter what he did, he couldn't find the right path. At the end of three days, he seemed to be deeper in the forest than when he started. Near exhaustion and close to hunger, he sat on a rock, his heart heavy with despair. Suddenly he saw a ragged man with a walking stick, obviously a woodsman himself.

The hiker explained his situation.

"I can't get out of the woods," he said. "Every path I take takes me deeper and deeper. I want to get home."

The woodsman was moved by the story.

"How long have you been lost?" he asked gently.

"Three whole days," the hiker cried. "I've walked and run, slashed the brush, cut down trees. I beg you, show me the way out of the forest."

"You've been lost for three days, you say? Well, just look at me," the woodsman said, pointing out his disheveled appearance. "I've been wandering in this forest for ten years! And I still haven't been able to find my way out of the tangle."

The hiker then burst into tears.

"When I saw you, I thought for sure that you could show me the way home. Now I know. There is no hope. Everything is lost."

The woodsman replied. "I don't think so. You *have* gained something from me. I have wandered for ten years, so I can at least teach you one thing of great value. I can show you which paths *don't* lead out of the woods."

The woodsman also knew the basics of survival. After all, he had been there for years. So the hiker had something else important to learn—what mushrooms to avoid, how to locate clean water, and how to make a shelter. With these basics in hand, he may well find his way out himself.

So what do you need to know? Where do you turn to find your way out of the ethical wilderness? Read on, and you'll start seeing the signs to help you find your way.

# 2

# The Basics

## The Need for Definitions

No matter how much we might wish otherwise, simple, straight-forward answers to ethical problems often are not possible. Even the Ten Commandments, the Western world's touchstone of Jewish and Christian ethics, need interpretation, as they offer broad principles of conduct rather than specific instructions. What does "Thou shall not kill" really mean? Only pacifists believe it to mean not killing ever, under any circumstances. Most people accept self-defense as justifiable homicide. In fact, the original intent of the commandment was to forbid the taking of innocent lives. What about stopping violence against others? Catholicism, for one, has developed a complex theory regarding just wars, taking the position that under certain circumscribed conditions soldiers of one army may kill soldiers of another.

Or take another commandment, "Thou shall not bear false witness against thy neighbor." This is generally taken to mean that you shouldn't lie. But what about so-called white lies, those social lubricants used to spare another's feelings? What about telling lies to enemies or to spare another's life? A widely used book on police interrogation, for example, urges police to use deceit, deception, and outright lies to trick suspects into confessing. (The point of baiting questions can introduce nonexistent evidence to a suspect as a means of evoking the truth.) In other words, police are encouraged to tell lies in order to get suspects to tell what the police believe is the truth.

In times past, some religious thinkers claimed that an utterance was not a lie if it was spoken for the promotion of Christianity. One interpretation of God's commandment to Abraham to kill his only son is that God was only testing Abraham's faith; he didn't really intend to have the father kill the son. If you tell someone one thing but mean another, even for good cause, you are deceiving them and lying to them. In that sense, God lied to Abraham to make a larger point.

In the above examples, questions of definition enter. What is killing? What is lying? We need to relate all commandments to particular circumstances, to specify what they intend to mean. It is for this reason that Judaism has produced commentaries upon commentaries, and Catholicism has a long-standing scholarly tradition in ethical theory and a method by which to decide ethical questions. It is why two believing Protestants can read the same scripture and reach different conclusions regarding its meaning and application. The Muslim, Buddhist, and Confucian traditions, too, have their libraries of scholarly works, teasing out the ethical implications of everyday affairs.

Pressing questions may not fit the preformed answers. So clergy, too, must use moral insights and reason to be helpful. Otherwise they will be like the minister who had two congregants come to him with a dispute. He listened to the first and said, "You're right." He listened to the second and said, "*You're* right." A friend who overheard the exchange said, "First you said one was right, then you said the other was right. They both can't be right." The minister responded, "You're right, too!"

"Okay," someone may say to me. "You're interested in ethics.

That's fine for you. But why should I care?" One answer is that we can't avoid morality no matter what we do. All of us are moralists. The difference is whether we pay attention to that fact or simply accept what others tell us to do. Another reason ethics is important is that we may rationalize our behavior and convince ourselves that something is right just because it favors us.

There was a time in my life when it was clear what the right thing to do was. I remember when my wife and I were living in Kenya as Peace Corps volunteers. My wife was pregnant, and several weeks before her due date she went to Nairobi to be under medical supervision required by the Peace Corps. I set out to join her at an outdoor café where we had arranged to meet. When I saw her sitting there sipping her coffee under an arching thorn tree, at first my heart leaped with joy, but when I came closer, something in me sank. Instead of enthusiasm, I felt something more like dread. Of course, I was glad to see my pregnant wife. At the same time, I knew for certain that my life would forever be changed. I was now to enter the ranks of the obligated. A person— a helpless creature, completely vulnerable and dependent—would be mine to protect. I couldn't leave or walk out or turn my back. My fate was sealed. With my newly acquired role as father, I would be bound to another in a way I never had been before. I wondered what this meant for my independence, how it affected my life goals, how much I would have to sacrifice because of my child. Even asking these questions made me feel self-centered, immature.

My reaction could be analyzed psychologically. But in another significant way, this situation could be understood from a moral point of view. For people in a traditional culture, such as the Kenyan one, many such questions wouldn't arise. Or perhaps more accurately, no one would ask them aloud. Roles were clearly spelled out, and society strictly enforced them. Indeed, morals have their roots in the customs of a culture. What it means to do the right thing is to follow the customs of the tribe. Only the courageous or crazy challenge this. Everyone knows what it means to be a father, everyone knows what is expected of him. Few agonize over trying to balance what is good for themselves with what is owed to others. If a person does not fulfill society's expectations, he or she suffers from social ostracism or worse.

The luxury of knowing without doubt what I ought to do—if that is what it was—was not possible for me. During my own lifetime, I witnessed a shift in what it means to be a father. I saw that my father's relationship to me was not the same as his father's to him. Grandpa was of the Old World, stern and distant, the mustachioed patriarch demanding if not respect, then obedience. Grandpa and Grandma didn't share affection as much as fate. But my parents married after courting. Companionship counted for something. I had choices that even my parents did not. Divorce for them was only a remote possibility. In my time, it is as prevalent as marriage itself. Those very same choices led to my unease, the uncertainty of not knowing what to do, what I *ought* to do as a father, as a husband. What were my responsibilities, most especially to the one most vulnerable, my baby?

## Moral Uncertainty

Life in modern-day America, and increasingly elsewhere throughout the world, offers no assurances regarding what is the morally correct thing to do. Today, three decades after my self-questioning, Kenyans, too, find that customs that held for centuries no longer quite apply. Children go to school and move away from home. At school they meet future mates of their own choosing, and no longer have parents selecting their spouse for them. They may well marry a person from a different ethnic group who has different customs. They, like us, find that modern life provides for material comforts but in return exacts the price of uncertainty and social instability.

Don't think that moral confusion is new. It isn't. Socrates tried to teach the young how to lead a virtuous life by taking no assumption for granted, by questioning nearly everything—an approach to moral education considered so subversive that he was condemned to death for such teaching. The twelfth-century Jewish scholar Maimonides, finding that existing texts didn't sufficiently address themselves to contemporary worries, wrote *The Guide for the Perplexed*. What is new is that more and more of us live in metropolitan settings where conflicting values come into play. Or if we aren't city dwellers ourselves, we are exposed to a variety of moral codes through the mass media that now reach around the world. Our ancestors would be just as uncertain as we are if they lived in today's society.

Some turn to a single text for answers, a clear-cut, no-nonsense guide. But which book? After Socrates' death, two of his students took divergent paths. Plato and Aristotle disagreed about ethics, the former believing in eternal values and the latter in the need for judgment in particular situations. Jesus broke with the Jewish establishment of his time, placing the spirit of the law above a strict interpretation of it, emphasizing motive over consequence.

Of course, there were people in traditional societies who were bothered by uncertainty and moral conflict. Abraham had to choose between disobeying God and taking the life of his son. Antigone had to choose between the laws of the state and the religious and familial duty to bury her brother. It may be more urgent, however, for us today than ever before, because so few customs exist upon which everyone agrees. Daily we come into instant contact with events ten thousand miles away via television and the Internet. This is a time of mass migrations and millions of displaced persons and refugees, a world in which representatives from nearly every nation meet in one building to discuss common problems.

Not everything we do hinges on morality, not every situation is an ethical one. Some decisions are nonmoral, as in deciding upon a particular flavor of ice cream. Some matters are at bottom psychological. If someone asks, "Why am I addicted to alcohol?" she is raising a psychobiological question that confronts motivation, cause, and effect. If the person asks, "How do I stop from drinking?" she is raising a practical question. But if the person asks, "Ought I to stop drinking?" she is asking a moral question. Ethical considerations arise when we try to evaluate our actions in terms of "right" or "good." Was this the right thing to do? Was it a good thing to do?

In the drinking example, the question becomes ethical when the person wonders whether drinking is desirable. Certainly, the person desires to drink. The implicit question is, are all desires worthy of indulging; that is, is that which is desired desirable? To answer this question, a series of other questions must be considered, such as: What effect does drinking have upon the person? How does it affect her health and character? What effect does it have upon others? Is this the best way to spend money? What pleasures are solitary and private? Whose business is it, anyway, that the person chooses to drink? The simple question "Ought I to stop drinking?" is entangled in a web of other questions that become progressively philosophical and abstract. Yet the question remains embedded in a real situation and the answers demand particular actions having real consequences in the lives of real people.

Many life decisions are, at least in part, ethical ones. The choices we might face regarding work, for example, have multiple moral dimensions. Here are some examples: deciding upon a fair salary; deciding whether to do everything asked of us; figuring out what to do with confidentially acquired information; understanding to what extent we have a right to privacy; deciding upon the extent to which we compromise in order to keep our jobs; understanding our responsibility to our coworkers; balancing what we owe to our place of employment with what we owe to our families; deciding whether our work is meaningful, or whether it is even important to engage in meaningful work; understanding in what way our work contributes to or hinders the welfare of others.

# Being Sensitive

These questions are important to those who are sensitive to the lives of others. Fortunately, there is a kernel somewhere inside most that responds to the misfortunes of strangers. Some studies indicate that the sound of an infant crying is enough to cause other infants to cry. When toddlers see another person, child or adult, in distress, they go over to offer comfort. It seems our capacity for empathy is inborn. Why some lose it as adults remains puzzling. Maybe out of self-interest we willfully turn away; perhaps our society breeds it out of us. Whatever the reason, happily, most adults still care.

Understanding morality as an emotional response to others in need leads to the conclusion that in a significant way, morality rests upon feelings. This has led some to say that ethics is therefore nothing more than feelings, and no more subject to reason than is one's preferences in ice cream flavors. But saying that morality requires sensitivity is not the same as saying that ethics is nothing more than feelings. Being sensitive to others, in other words, is a necessary but not sufficient condition for doing the right thing. Not only do we need to recognize that something is wrong, we still need to know what to do.

# 3

# A Little Theory

## Three Approaches to Ethics

Who wants theory anyhow? Can't we just get on with the problems? We could, and most people do. After all, most of us can operate a computer without knowing anything about how it works. But it can be helpful to understand some theory. It can make solving the problems that confront us easier. I'm not an auto mechanic, and if I put my hands on a tool, I'm bound to make things worse. But I know a little bit of the theory about how cars work, so when my car has a problem I know whether I should take care of it immediately or whether it can wait. My knowledge also protects me from being taken advantage of by an unscrupulous mechanic.

If you know just a little theory, you will make better ethical decisions. You will have a framework within which to decide what to do. So here is the theory in a nutshell.

There are three basic types of ethical theories: one, virtue ethics; two, consequentialist ethics; and three, principled ethics. These are systematic ways of thinking about moral issues. While there are subdivisions within these groups, you can think of each as a cluster of thought or a school of moral philosophy.

Let's take a look at the three leading schools of thought, variations of which can be found around the world. As you read through them, ask yourself which one makes the most sense to you. Do you have a preference? Why? Think of a moral problem you have had and which moral course you decided was right. Which of these three approaches did you actually use in making your decision?

Virtue ethics, which focuses upon character, is the most ancient of the three types. Aristotle is perhaps the most famous proponent of this way of thinking about ethical matters. Those who look at ethics through the lens of character ask, "What sort of person should I aim to be and what do I need to do to fulfill that goal?" The main point of this approach is individual integrity.

In virtue ethics, acting true to oneself and fulfilling the goals of life are what it means to be a full human being. A person who accepts the virtue approach to ethics is moved to action because acting as a virtuous person is the only way he can live with himself. This approach to ethics had fallen into disuse by philosophers for a century or more, only to be revived in the latter part of the twentieth century by Alasdair MacIntyre, who wrote a book called *After Virtue*. People who are concerned with character education for children often use this approach to ethics.

Those who employ the consequentialist (or empirical) basis for morality focus on psychological traits such as affection, sympathy, a moral sense, intuition, and so forth. Perhaps the earliest leading philosopher of this approach is Scotsman David Hume. Since empiricists are observing things as they are, they are led to ask the question, "What is the result of what I do?"

Those who look to results are concerned less with the kind of a person someone is than with the outcome of the actions the person takes. In Europe this approach stresses the greatest good for the greatest number of people—the utilitarian theory. The

U.S. form of this school is philosophical pragmatism, an approach that values results over principles and looks toward producing the desired outcome.

The third group or school thinks that ethics must be based on principles that are certain and universal. A principled approach to ethics relies upon rationality and obligates a person to live consistently with what reason requires. The German Immanuel Kant is the leading philosopher here. Those who base their ethics upon principle and rationality and search for valid generalizations ask, "What does reason morally require me to do?" "Duty" and "ought" are terms frequently employed in this ethical system, which seeks universal principles that apply to all people, everywhere, all the time.

## Each Theory Is Limited

The problem with virtue ethics is that it isn't clear what set of virtues are most important. Aristotle and the Greeks had theirs—wisdom, courage, temperance, and justice; Thomas Aquinas and the Christians had theirs—faith, hope, and charity. The Chinese produced a slightly different set, and so forth. A virtue is like a target—you aim at it and try to reach the mark. But it begs the question as to which target you should be aiming at. Virtue ethics has the disadvantage of being culture bound. What it holds up as virtue turns out often to be a reflection of conventional morality—what is right is right because society says it's right. This is not much help in situations in which there is a conflict of values or where society's morality itself seems to be immoral. Virtue ethics becomes a relativistic ethic: everything depends upon the culture in which one lives.

Consequentialist ethics is limited because it severs results from the way in which the results were obtained. It looks primarily at outcomes, not input. Only the ends are important, not the means by which they were achieved. The problem is twofold: first, measuring ethics only by its consequences overlooks the fact that a bad person may produce something worthwhile as a by-product of some evil; and second, it can't distinguish between, say, a student who gets an A honestly and one who gets it by cheating. Consequentialist ethics can be reduced to a crude utilitarianism—if it works, it's good, and the greatest good for the greatest number is what is important, no matter how one arrives at producing that good. It may also suffer from a rough cultural relativism in which no judgments can be made about other groups. In a class on human rights I taught, many students refused to admit that torture was bad. All they wanted to say was that torture was immoral in America but that it may not be immoral elsewhere in the world.

The third ethical school, in which morality is built upon rational principle, also has its limitations. Taken to their logical and extreme conclusion, principles can lead to inhumane results, for they can ignore probable consequences of our actions.

In the fairy tale "Beauty and the Beast," for example, the father, in return for his own release, promises the Beast that he will bring him in exchange the first living thing he sees upon returning home. This turns out not to be a domestic animal, as he had hoped, but his daughter Beauty. A promise is a promise after all, and in good principled fashion, Father convinces Beauty to go to the Beast's home to be imprisoned. Father could forswear the promise—it was made under extortion and the consequences of keeping it are extreme, two mitigating considerations—but he doesn't, so an innocent life is potentially sacrificed for the sake of keeping one's word. This is what can happen with such scrupulous adherence to a principled morality. It is a logical absurdity.

# What to Consider

Philosophers argue among themselves which of the three approaches is correct. They have little patience with the person who will sometimes use one, then another concept. But I believe that it is the person who struggles with these perplexities who comes closer to the reality of things than do those who insist on a unitary moral system. Different people in all good faith can reach different conclusions about ethical matters, because they each may be employing a different one of the three ethical systems. But to make matters even more complex, we can disagree with one another because of a whole set of other contingencies. Here are some of the factors that need attention:

Every time you confront a situation, you have to decide on the *facts* of the case. (Is someone lying or telling the truth?) Next you have to *interpret* the facts. (Did the person have cause to lie?) Then you have to fill in the gaps in the story with *assumptions*, if you can't ask the protagonist directly. (Did the person mean to lie?) On top of this you overlay your own set of *values*. (How important is the matter?) Then you go about prizing one ethical *principle* over another. (How important is telling the truth?) This makes for at least eight variables (three ethical systems, facts, interpretation, assumptions, values, and principles) that you employ when you make an ethical decision. So, leaving aside psychological variations, such as temperament, a mathematician friend tells me that this mix of variables presents nearly two hundred possible ways in which people of goodwill and serious thought can disagree with one another over moral matters.

One reason for the divergence is that ethical theory often uses only rational considerations, divorced from psychological, cultural, political, and social realities. The life you lead, the meaning you attribute to it, and the manner in which you experience them are more complicated than any unitary theory can contain. No one is a perfect type or singly motivated. You may be inconsistent or contradictory. Ralph Waldo Emerson said, "A foolish consistency is the hobgoblin of little minds." And Walt Whitman exclaimed, "Do I contradict myself? Very well then I contradict myself. (I am large, I contain multitudes.)"

But most of us also lean in one direction or another. Who knows, we may even be born with certain proclivities. Recent studies involving twins and triplets separated at birth indicate that their likes and dislikes are far closer to those of their biological siblings than of their adoptive families. Although raised apart, they share tastes in jokes, clothing, music, dating partners, and so forth. The adoptive families have little effect in this area.

Still, while we may be inclined in one direction or the other, we still make choices that are under our control. This is what it means to be an ethical person.

# 4

~~❦~~

# Ethical Judgments

## Ethics and Good Judgment

The real issue in ethics isn't taste or inclination or preference. It is developing an ethical approach to living, whichever method of justification you use. This goes to the heart of morality. Aristotle called it a combination of action, desire, and feeling. This requires the use of judgment so that you may apply what you believe to be right to the situation at hand. Having ethical principles alone isn't enough. As legal scholar and philosopher David Luban explains, moral decision-making "also requires good judgment, by which I mean knowing which actions violate a moral principle and which do not." He continues, "You can't teach good judgment through general rules, because you already need judgment to know how rules apply." His conclusion applies to the point of this book. "Judgment is therefore always and irredeemably particular."

In ethics you are one of the subjects of your own inquiry. If an ethical life matters to you, you must already be committed to particular values and principles. You therefore inevitably view things through your own interests and experiences. All of us are products of biology, history, and social institutions, each of which shapes our understanding and beliefs regarding what it means to be human.

In ethics, reason can never be divorced from the particularity of individual lives. Ethics is difficult precisely because it is so close and matters so much.

To make matters worse still, morality sometimes claims too much of us. There is always something more we could be doing to make the world a better place—more help to give a friend, another good cause to support. Sometimes a conflict arises in our values, or a gap appears between our ideals and our behavior. Knowing that we have failed to fully live up to an ethical standard leaves the silt of self-recrimination. By being less than we think we ought to be—that is, less than perfect—we feel guilty and maybe even ashamed, emotions that, when unchecked, make living the moral life less likely, not more likely.

If ethics were all there was to life, there would be no leisure, no projects of our own. Life would be a chore to complete instead of a joy to be experienced. If ethics makes demands, you may believe, it must make demands absolutely, without exception and on all people under the same circumstances, the same way.

But moral obligation is only one type of ethical consideration. Fortunately, this is not all there is to ethics. Living a good life, too, is part of an ethical outlook. This means that while obligations to others are very important, they aren't the only thing. You need to remember this, particularly if you are frequently drawn between those who, on the one hand, claim that there is only one right way, only one righteous path, and those who, on the other hand, maintain that ethics is nothing but the hollow call for conformity by authority.

## There's No Choice but to Choose

Undoubtedly, ethics is a difficult subject. But it is not the only difficult subject. I remember little about geometry and care hardly at all that others do the thinking for me in that subject. But I know that such a choice regarding ethics would be a personal disaster. The Greek philosopher Epicurus explained why. "Let no one when young delay to study philosophy, nor when he is old grow weary of his study. For no one can come too early or too late to secure the health of his soul."

To secure the health of our souls, we need to turn to a variety of sources. An analogy with physical health is instructive. In the past, few gave much thought to the food they ate. Buttered biscuits, sausages, candy, and ice cream—all delicious but deadly in large amounts. Now we know that exercise and what we put into our mouths affect our health. Yet we may still be confused by all the information available to us. Running is good for us—running ruins the knees; red meat is bad for us—red meat provides essential nutrients; sunlight is a healing agent for depression—sunlight causes cancer.

Ethics confronts us in a similar manner. Many voices compete for our attention, each persuading, cajoling, hectoring, demanding that we do the right thing. However, just as with health issues, we can turn to others for moral guidance. First, we sift the quacks from the serious, using our intelligence, experience, imagination, and emotions to decide the difference. We read what we can from the wisdom of the world's religions, and we try to understand the great ethical philosophers who have contributed to our heritage. Next, we look to contemporary guides, people whose judgment we trust, those who seem to be examples of what they preach. We talk and discuss, we listen and argue. Then we try as best we can to understand all the relevant facts about the issue in front of us. We use our conscience, paying close attention to how we feel, what we think, what we believe. Finally, we take the interests of others into account, attempting to understand the world through the eyes of those most likely to be affected by our action. Then we apply our judgment.

As with the food we eat, unavoidably we are the final arbiter. We cannot escape this responsibility. This is a bother, but there is no other route as long as we are concerned with the health of our souls.

Sometimes we are confronted with competing claims, each important in its own right. One can even imagine situations where the claims upon us are equal and equally important. Jean Paul Sartre imagined such a drama when he wrote about a young man during World War II who was the only caretaker for his chronically ill mother. The Nazis were approaching his town. He was needed by the Resistance to help defeat the invaders. But if he went to fight the noble and necessary cause, his mother would die.

Facing ethical choices may discourage us from choosing at all. But choice itself is built into the human condition. Ants don't decide between love and justice, human life and art. They live by instincts alone. Humans are different. Instincts may guide us on the most basic level—hungry, eat; tired, sleep; frightened, run away. Yet even here there are choices: eat what and sleep where? And we all know that running away when endangered may not always be a good idea. I learned in the army that when a land mine blew up next to me, I should stay still, figure out was going on, then act.

So we must choose or someone else will choose for us. Even not to choose is a choice—sometimes a good and wise thing to do, sometimes not. The point is to be aware of our choices and to act in the best way possible.

# 5

❦

# Finding a Way to Decide

## Steps to Take

Amy Gutmann and Dennis Thompson, two political philosophers, offer an approach to ethical problems that they call "standards of deliberation." First, every appeal to reason or principles you use must be one that could be accepted by other reasonable people. This means that there must be a degree of consistency, coherence, and logic to what you say. Second, the factual claims you make must be testable by reliable and nonprivate methods. You can't say something like "You broke my arm," but not let anyone see your arm. You have to allow your arm to be seen and examined by those who know what broken arms are. You can't refuse to share information your have or claim something as fact just because it "feels right" or because "I said so." Third, all your reasons must be offered in public. You shouldn't solve ethical problems based on secret information. This is unfair to others, as it puts them at a disadvantage.

More specifically, here is a series of steps you can use in making an ethical decision:

1. What are the facts? Know the facts as best you can. If your facts are wrong, you're liable to make a bad choice.

2.  What can you guess about the facts you don't know? Since it is impossible to know all the facts, make reasonable assumptions about the missing pieces of information.

3.  What do the facts mean? Facts by themselves have no meaning. You need to interpret the information in light of the values that are important to you.

4.  What does the problem look like through the eyes of the various people involved? The ability to walk in another's shoes is essential. Understanding the problem through a variety of perspectives increases the possibility that you will choose wisely.

5.  What will happen if you choose one thing rather than another? All actions have consequences. Make a reasonable guess as to what will happen if you follow a particular course of action. Decide whether you think more good or harm will come of your action.

6.  What do your feelings tell you? Feelings are facts, too. Your feelings about ethical issues may give you a clue as to parts of your decision that your rational mind may overlook.

7.  What will you think of yourself if you decide one thing or another? Some call this your conscience. It is a form of self-appraisal. It helps you decide whether you are the kind of person you would like to be. It helps you to live with yourself.

8.  Can you explain and justify your decision to others? Your behavior shouldn't be based on a whim. Neither should it be self-centered. Ethics involves you in the life of the world around you. For this reason, you must be able to justify your moral decisions in ways that seem reasonable to reasonable people. Ethical reasons can't be private reasons.

In the early twentieth century, the great American ethical philosopher Morris Raphael Cohen wrote that without moral choice "there is no genuinely human life, but only slavish adherence to mechanically rigid rules which choke the currents of ever-changing life." The choice, then, is between thinking things out for ourselves, judging and acting on those ethical values—however uncertain we may be about them—or living like slaves, afraid of risks, waiting for someone else to tell us what to do. While we have a moral vocabulary from which to construct our answers, there is no text, which by itself can tell what is right or wrong for each and every situation. Knowing this and acting nevertheless is the essence of responsibility and free will.

# PART TWO

# Your Moral Intelligence

6

⤛❦⤜

# Improving Your Moral IQ

## Caring

Ethical philosophers and many religious leaders think about morality all the time. What is right? What is wrong? What values should guide our lives? What do you owe others? What is fair? What does it mean to be good? What is a good life? These, and questions like them, become their life work.

How does someone become a good person? When asked this question, Aristotle answered by counseling one to find a virtuous person and watch what he does. This is still good advice, as far as it goes. Imitation has its limits, though, since you see only what a person does but not why he does it. Why sacrifice yourself for the sake of a friend? Why return something that you have found? Why fulfill a promise even if it is costly to you?

Once you ask, "Why should I do this instead of that?" you are in the realm of judgment. And here psychologists have something to tell you about how and why people make the moral choices they do. Obviously, it has something to do with how you are raised. If you have confidence in yourself, you probably have the courage of your convictions. If you were raised in a home with respect, you can extend respect to others. But your childhood is literally in the past. Is there anything you can do now to help raise the level of your ethical competence?

The answer is yes. First, in the area of caring and compassion, reading fiction, history, and biographies can make people more sensitive to the lives of others. Literature of this sort connects you to others in a way that helps you see the world through their eyes. This is the first step. Without care nothing else can happen.

# Judging

The second thing you can do is to think about ethical problems. There are increasing levels of sophistication in reasoning about ethics. Many psychologists accept the schema arranged by Lawrence Kohlberg in which he outlined five stages of moral development. The first stage claims that the reason for doing the right thing is to avoid punishment. The second stage argues that the right thing is that which serves your own interests. The third stage argues that you do the right thing so others will think well of you. The fourth stage reasons that you do the right thing in order that society as a whole can function. The fifth stage accepts the right thing as that which promotes the welfare of all people and protects everyone's rights.

The better you reason, the more morally competent you are. This is much like saying that the better you understand math, the better mathematician you are. Of course, you can occasionally guess the right answer, and there are idiot savants who do amazing mathematical feats without having a clue how they arrived at the right answers. Furthermore, you can know everything you need to know about math and choose never to balance your checkbook. I assume, though, if you've gotten this far in the book, you are interested in "doing ethics."

# Taking a Test and Talking

A way to improve your level of reasoning about ethics is to discuss ethical problems with other people, rather than simply to think about them on your own. Moral development is spurred by your hearing other thoughtful responses to moral problems. Reflection best takes place when you know what others think and you explain your reasoning to other thoughtful people.

Following are five stories describing dilemmas for you to think about. Answer the question following the stories. Find other people who are willing to read the stories and talk about their answers with you. Go over your responses and explain why you ranked them the way you did. You can think of other stories to discuss when you are done with these. Ethical problems are all around us. Hardly a day goes by that an ethical dilemma doesn't confront you. Nearly every day you can find a moral issue in the news.

Remember, there aren't any right or wrong answers. But some answers are more comprehensive, more inclusive of ethical considerations, than other responses. So unlike some other self-improvement quizzes, there is no final score here. There's no number you can derive that says whether you are an ethical person. Being ethical is more than making good ethical judgments—it means doing what a good ethical person does, and judging is only one part of that.

But there is a way of looking at the answers you have given that focuses on ethical judgments and gives you some sense of where you stand in this regard. I will explain what I mean following story number five, in the section titled "Evaluation."

Meanwhile, go ahead and take the quiz, either alone or with others. Either way, it's challenging, stimulating, and fun.

# An Ethical Quiz

## STORY 1

Paula is a forty-year-old woman who lives in New York City and has had cancer for several years. She has undergone chemotherapy as well as radiation. In addition, she has endured several operations. Her doctor now reports that the cancer has reoccurred and there is no other treatment for her. He expects that she has about six months to live.

Meanwhile, Paula has read about a doctor in Mexico who claims to have a high success rate in treating Paula's kind of cancer with an herbal remedy. When she asks her doctor about it, he tells her that there is no scientific basis for the treatment. Not only is it an unorthodox treatment but it is also illegal in the United States.

Paula is too sick to travel to Mexico herself. She calls the doctor there and is told that he won't mail the medication but that it must be obtained in person. However, he tells her, if she can't come herself he will give it to someone she has authorized.

Paula phones her friend John in San Diego and asks if he would go to Tijuana, just a few miles away, and get the medication for her. John arranges to get the drug for Paula in Mexico, then mails it to her from his home in San Diego.

1. Do you think John did the right thing in getting the drug for Paula?
2. If you think he did, why do you think so?
3. If you think he didn't, why not?
4. Do you think that John's friendship to Paula is enough for him to break the law?

5. Do you think that following the law was more important than helping Paula?
6. Do you think that Paula was right in asking John?
7. If you think she was right, why?
8. If you think she was wrong, why?
9. What do you see as the most important ethical value in this case?
10. What do you think is the major ethical conflict?

On a scale of one to five, with five being the highest, give John an ethical score.

## STORY 2

Colleen is the president of the board of a drug and alcohol rehabilitation treatment program. While the program is part of a private not-for-profit agency, nearly all of the program's funds come from the county, and the government provides oversight through audits.

In the past year the agency's budget has doubled and as a result the county has required that the agency hire a professional bookkeeper. The county recommends Frank, a recent college graduate. Colleen knows that Barbara, recently retired as a bookkeeper, is interested in working for the agency.

The board reviews both applications and decides to offer the position to Barbara. The chief of finances from the county tells Colleen that Barbara isn't an acceptable choice and insists they hire Frank instead. The board compares the credentials of both candidates again and once more concludes that Barbara is the better choice.

The county representative is adamant. He tells Colleen that if the agency hires Barbara instead of Frank, the county will cut off next year's funds. Without the money the agency will have to close.

Colleen is told that Frank is the nephew of the county's chief of finances. Other board members complain about the county's interference in the running of not only this agency but of others in the area. It is well known that many of the county jobs are patronage positions.

Colleen suggests that the board insist on hiring Barbara even if it means the agency will go broke within a year and votes this way when a motion is made to that effect.

1. Do you think that Colleen was right in voting this way?
2. If you do, why do you think she did the right thing?
3. If you don't, why not?
4. Do you think that following a principle was more impor-tant than keeping the agency going?
5. Do you think that Colleen was foolish in risking the well-being of all the clients for the sake of a principle?
6. What do you see as the most important ethical value in this case?
7. What do you think is the major ethical conflict?

On a scale of one to five, with five being the highest, give Colleen an ethical score.

## STORY 3

Alicia is a history professor. She is highly student-cen-tered: she cares about her students, she makes herself available beyond her office hours, and she works with stu-dents individually outside of class. She has a reputation for being fair. However, she also has a clear policy regarding class attendance and participation.

At the end of the semester she gives Julian a D. She

reached this decision after reviewing his work several times and factoring in many absences. After the grades are posted, Julian makes an appointment to see Alicia. He explains that he is a member of the football team and is at school on an athletic scholarship. He comes from a poor family that can't otherwise send him to college. He very much wants to stay in school but can't keep his scholarship with a D. He must receive C's or better in all his classes. He asks if there is anything Alicia can do to help him raise his grade.

Alicia reviews his record again and concludes that she had been generous in not failing him in the first place. The best she can do for him is to raise his grade to a C-. With that grade, Julian would still lose his scholarship.

Alicia also knows that if she doesn't give Julian the C, she will receive pressure from the athletic director. It turns out that Julian is the star player of the team.

Alicia refuses to raise his grade any higher.

1. Do you think Alicia did the right thing?
2. If you do, why do you think she did the right thing?
3. If not, why not?
4. Do you think standards should be applied equally to all students?
5. Do you think standards should be flexible to meet the needs of individual students?
6. Do you think Alicia was being foolish in risking her job because of the decision she made?
7. What do you see as the most important ethical value in this case?
8. What do you think is the major ethical conflict?

On a scale of one to five, with five being the highest, give Alicia an ethical score.

## STORY 4

Melissa is self-employed as a public relations consultant with four main clients. A large part of her work is sending out press releases for the various organizations. Like many consultants she works from home at her own pace, keeps track of her own hours, and gets paid by the job as estimated by the amount of time it takes her to do the work.

Melissa has been consulting for one organization for about ten years. Since she began working for them she has bought a computer, learned how to use it adeptly, and recently upgraded to a faster model.

She is now able to fax press releases using the computer. She simply writes a release, uses an existing list of newspapers she has compiled, and lets the computer do the rest. What used to take ten hours now takes her less than an hour of her own time. The computer time is another two hours.

Melissa decides not to tell the organizations she works for that she now no longer takes as much time doing the job as she did in the past and continues to charge them the same amount.

1. Do you think Melissa did the right thing?
2. If you do, why do you think it was right?
3. If not, why not?
4. Do you think she was obliged to disclose the information to her clients?
5. Do you think she would be foolish if she charged them less for the work?
6. What do you see as the most important ethical value in this case?
7. What do you think is the major ethical conflict?

On a scale of one to five, with five being the highest, give Melissa an ethical score.

## STORY 5

Emily and Jim have a son, and they plan to adopt a daughter. When the home evaluation begins, they are living in an apartment. The social worker interviews them and observes their son. Everything about Emily and Jim make them ideal adoptive parents.

A year later the social worker comes for a final interview. By this time, Emily and Jim have moved from their two-bedroom apartment to a three-bedroom house. During the interview, the social worker asks to see the bedroom that will be their new daughter's room. They show her their son's room. The social worker explains that the girl must have a room of her own because agency policy requires that children of the opposite sex be separated.

Emily and Jim have a private conversation and then tell the social worker that they had planned to have the children share the same bedroom until they were older. But Emily and Jim thought it was best for the children to share a room while they were young.

The social worker encourages Emily and Jim to say that they would have separate rooms for the children and they could do as they wish later on. Emily and Jim tell the social worker that if she wants them to lie they will, but that she should know they aren't telling her the truth.

In her report, the social worker writes that the two children would be using the same bedroom.

1. Do you think Emily and Jim did the right thing?
2. If you do, why do you think it was right?
3. If not, why not?
4. Do you think the social worker did the right thing?
5. If you do, why do you think it was right?
6. If not, why not?
7. Do you think it was foolish of Emily and Jim to have done what they did?
8. Do you think the social worker was being fair to the family for having written the report as she did?
9. What do you see as the most important ethical value in this case?
10. What do you see as the major ethical conflict?

On a scale of one to five, with five being the highest, give Emily and Jim an ethical score.

On a scale of one to five, with five being the highest, give the social worker an ethical score.

## STORY 6

Stewart worked as a detective for many years. Over the years he developed many sources both in government and in industry. When he retired, he decided to work for a private company involved in industrial espionage.

Stewart's work involves gathering information about people such as their social security numbers, investment portfolios, bank accounts, and credit history. He carefully follows the law in obtaining his information.

One day he is asked to work on a big and difficult case. The only way Stewart can obtain the information is by having one of his contacts violate a technicality in the law.

Stewart's contact provides him with the information and Stewart passes it on to his employer.

1. Do you think Stewart did the right thing?
2. If you do, why do you think it was right?
3. If not, why not?
4. Do you think Stewart would have been foolish not to use the information provided to him?
5. Do you think the law should be followed in all cases?
6. Do you think Stewart's contact should have refused to get the information requested?
7. What do you see as the most important ethical value in this case?
8. What do you see as the major ethical conflict?

On a scale of one to five, with five being the highest, give Stewart an ethical score.

## Evaluation

There is no right or wrong answer for this dilemma. It isn't whether Stewart passes on the information to his employer, for example, but the reasons you think he should or shouldn't. It is the set of questions that follows each story that is most important.

Look at the questions following the six stories. You may notice that while the questions following each story are specific to it, there are recurring themes that run through all six sets.

The questions are designed to look at where you may fit on the Kohlberg scale of moral development. Remember, not all psychologists or philosophers accept this approach. For one thing, it only examines your ideas about ethics. It says nothing about what you might do in real life, although there is a strong indication that a link exists between ethical judgments and behavior in real life. But we all know exceptions to this rule, so view it with a grain of salt.

The Kohlberg scheme constructs five stages of moral development, described earlier in the chapter in the section titled "Judging." The questions are prompts to see which of the stages you prefer. Therefore, some of your answers may center on avoiding punishment; other answers may be related to serving your own interests; others may reflect the desire to have people think well of you; some answers may stress the importance of maintaining social order; and other answers may be connected to the desire to promote the welfare of everyone.

You can see for yourself where you fall in terms of stages of moral judgments. It is important to take this test again when you have finished the book. Do you still prefer the same reasons? Have they changed? Why are they different?

PART THREE

❧

# Ethics with Family and Friends: Being Ethical to Those Closest to Me

Parts Three and Four contain a set of ethical case studies. After each vignette, I give you my response to it and whether I think the person did the right thing. I give you my reasons for reaching the conclusion I do. But I know that each problem is difficult and can be viewed in a variety of ways. So for each dilemma I've asked a different person also to respond. Sometimes the two of us agree. Sometimes we disagree—over facts, over interpretation, over values, over principles, over the prediction of what is going to happen.

The best way to read this section is to take one case at a time. Answer the questions I pose at the head of the vignette before reading the situation. Think it through for yourself. I don't want you to be biased by the discussion that follows. Be sure to make a note of whether you thought the person in the study did the moral thing.

Then read through the reactions, and when you are finished, go back and answer the questions again. Which arguments did you find most persuasive? Why? Do you understand the problem in a new way? Did you change your mind after your read the commentary?

Go on to the next problem and go through the same process. When you have finished all twenty-one dilemmas, think about the pattern that your answers form. Can you find a thread that holds them all together? Do you want to rethink anything?

As a final step in this section, find someone who will also go through the same process as you. If there are several of you, so much the better. Then have a discussion based upon each question, one at a time. Try to understand each other's reasoning, just as you tried to understand the reasons given by the respondent and me.

If you go through these steps, you are bound to improve your moral IQ, as discussion and reflection deepen your ability to make sound ethical judgments.

# 7

# Should I Always
# Keep a Confidence?

Dan, fifteen years old, enjoys talking to his friend's mother, Nicole. Many times he has confided his problems to her. Now he comes to the house to ask if he can talk to her confidentially. After she agrees, he tells her that he has saved enough money to run away. She tries to persuade him not to, but fails. As soon as Dan leaves her house, Nicole calls his parents to tell them of their son's plans.

Some questions to ask yourself:

1. Should you always keep a promise?
2. How do you decide what confidences to keep?
3. Is it legitimate to share another's confidences with someone in your family?
4. Is it okay to share confidences with another person who may help you?
5. Under what circumstances should a confidence be broken?
6. Does the age of the person who talks to you confidentially make a difference?
7. Is Nicole doing the right thing?

# The Problem:
# Does a Confidence
# Require Absolute Silence?

People confide in me all the time, sometimes as a friend, sometimes as a their teacher, sometimes as their counselor, and sometimes as their minister. Each time, I need to decide whether I can repeat all, some, or none of what is told to me. Of all my roles, the one that is easiest to put a fence around is that of clergy. I have no doubts that the conversation between a member of my congregation and me is not to be repeated to anyone under any circumstances, unless I get that person's permission to do so. I am reluctant to repeat a story to colleagues, even when the name is disguised and the presentation can serve a useful, educational purpose. My circumspection applies equally to my wife. She knows nothing about what any member of my Society has ever told me that in any way I construe to have been told to me in confidence. I cast my net wide, always assuming that the discussion is confidential unless the matter is truly trivial.

I do this because I believe that what someone tells me in my ministerial role is meant to stay just between the two of us. Without this implicit confidence, people are less likely to speak to their spiritual leaders with any degree of trust. In a sense, it is like thinking out loud. They assume that the room isn't bugged. People need to unburden themselves, to say the most awful things, to reveal the most hideous thoughts and the most heinous behavior. They do this not to feel better but to get guidance on how to go on with their lives. If they didn't believe that what they said would go no further, would they ever say it?

# Professional Confidentiality:
## The Need to Be Candid

Professionals such as doctors, lawyers, psychotherapists, social workers, and clergy place a high premium on confidentiality. By and large, the law even protects the privacy of conversations with these designated professionals. The courts legally exempt them from revealing information obtained during the course of performing their duties.

There is wisdom in this. People need to trust their doctors. They wouldn't be candid if they thought that information they gave a physician could be used against them. But the even the confidential relationship between patient and doctor has limits. For example, physicians must report to the police anyone who has been shot. The same goes for lawyers. Lawyers don't tell the judge what clients have told them in preparation for a defense. If they had to, they could not adequately defend the client, and therefore fair trials would be unobtainable. Yet lawyers, at least according to one of the codes of ethics that guide trial attorneys, must reveal perjuries committed by their clients. There also are limits for psychotherapists. In the landmark Tarasoff case, in California two decades ago, the court assessed liability against a psychotherapist for "failure to warn" a victim that his patient intended to murder her. The civil case found that there is a professional duty to protect a third party against harm.

# Professional Confidentiality:
## Serving Society's Interests

Confidentiality is a privilege extended to these categories of professionals because we believe that it best serves society's interests.

Without confidentiality, doctors may not be able treat their patients properly, or people might not come to them in the first place. This latter point has been the argument used in several states to prevent doctors from revealing the results for patients who test positive for AIDS. (The counterargument is that the public interest is best served by treating AIDS like other contagious and potentially deadly diseases, mainly by mandating reporting to public health officials.)

Shortly before he died, someone confessed to me a crime he had committed years before. He said that everyone thought that his alcoholic wife had died in an accident in the home. Actually, he couldn't bear her any longer so he killed her, making it look like an accident. He told me because he needed to assuage his guilt and die with a less burdened conscience. I don't think he would have told me the story if he thought that in any way I would betray his trust even after his death. Although he wouldn't be alive to know what I did with the information, it was important to him that it not be made public.

# Confidentiality: Respect for Human Dignity

Confidentiality, then, rests upon the assurance that we will not be betrayed. For this reason, one spouse cannot be made to testify against the other. (Oddly enough, this privilege isn't extended to parent-child relationships. I see no good reason why this should be so.) A good and stable marriage requires a high degree of trust, openness, and honesty. Totalitarian governments encourage family members to spy on one another, report deviant behavior or thought. Despots know that the ability to keep something secret is a form of power, and in dictatorships, no power is allowed other than that of the government. Confidentiality contributes to human dignity by protecting an individual from un-warranted intrusion.

Keeping someone's confidence is a sign that you respect him. He reveals something of himself to you, perhaps a secret, and you in turn protect what he has said. But sometimes keeping a secret and doing what is best for a person isn't the same thing. For example, a child talks to her teacher about beatings she receives at home. Is it really in the child's interest that the teacher not report this child abuse? Some states have decided that it is not, and have gone a step further. They have made it a crime *not* to report such allegations. As a matter of public policy and law, in New York, as elsewhere, a teacher cannot keep her student's confidence once the child has either talked about abuse or the teacher has a reasonable belief that such abuse has taken place. Teachers are not offered the shield of confidentiality that is extended to lawyers, for a lawyer who knows that a client has abused a child cannot report it since this would jeopardize the client's ability to receive a fair trial, something to which everyone in our society is entitled. But in the instance of children and teachers, in order to protect the child, government authorities invade a family's privacy.

# A Social Worker's Advice: The Initial Mistake

The story in this chapter, however, does not deal with either professional confidentiality or with family. So I asked a social worker what she thought of Nicole's actions. Joan Beder teaches social work ethics at Yeshiva University. She states that Nicole has made a couple of errors. "I would have hoped that Nicole would have stated the limitations of her interchanges with Dan, especially as he is only fifteen years old. She shouldn't have agreed to the conditions of confidentiality. Nicole, who was acting out of caring and generous motives, may have made a judgment error to freely assure Dan that his secret would be kept between them."

But that's past history. At this point Dan is talking to Nicole. What should she do then? "As a friend, which Nicole was to him, her best path would have been to try to understand his motivation to run away, empathize and console, and urge him to try to work things out with his family. Had I been Nicole," Beder says, "I would have urged Dan to attempt to reconcile with his parents, would have looked with him at his motives for running away, would have attempted to help him see where change could occur, where he might be able to work with his family rather than leaving them."

There are some lines of discussion that Beder would stay away from. "I would have tried to avoid what this would do to his parents in terms of their anguish and worry. This line of discussion might solidify his motivation to run away, as upset, anguish, and worry might be what he wishes for his parents. I would also have avoided talking about how upsetting this might be to Nicole's child, Dan's friend. Guilt does not seem to work too well under these circumstances, having the potential to fuel the anger of the individual rather than not."

If after listening to Nicole, Dan decides to run away anyhow, then what? Beder says, "As a friend, Nicole had an obligation to tell Dan's parents and protect him from making a poor decision. A friend often has to look out for their friend's welfare in complex ways. What Nicole was risking in calling Dan's parents was that she would most probably lose his trust and friendship. Dan might subsequently have difficulty trusting other adults in the future. But Dan is a troubled youngster, and the bonds of friendship and belief in what is best in the situation demand that action be taken. So the value of confidentiality is overridden by the knowledge of how disruptive Dan's running away would have been."

# Know What You Are Agreeing To

I agree with Beder. Nicole is right in judging that Dan's parents, not she, have the larger responsibility for Dan's welfare. To this extent she is correct. At the point at which Dan walks out of her house, it would be cruel for her to be indifferent to Dan's parents' frantic worry. Because she has talked to Dan and he trusts her, she cannot turn her back on him now. I would question her real motives about being Dan's confidant if she does nothing and leaves his parents in ignorance. Her duty to help Dan overrides her promise to him. No matter how strained his relationship may be with his parents, they must know. To feel bound by a promise of confidentiality is to place a principle above the interests of real people.

I also agree that Nicole's real problem stems from having agreed to listen to Dan under the conditions he set out in the first place. Much better would have been for her to say something like, "If you want to tell me something, fine. But I can't promise you that I'll keep it secret until I hear what you have to tell me." At that point, Dan may choose not to say anything and run away in any case. Then she would not even have the chance of talking him out of it. But if her relationship with him has really been a good one, she probably could get him to talk to her. With some gentle coaxing he might tell her what is bothering him so much that he feels he has to leave his family.

It is risky to agree to hold a confidence before you know what the person is asking. Too easily the secret becomes a manipulation; it makes the hearer impotent. To ask another to hold a confidence can be a tool of control. It is important to be able to count on the confidentiality of professionals, but in personal relations the real issue is trust between people. In the past, Dan has trusted Nicole—that's why he has talked to her. Nicole does nothing to enhance that trust by agreeing to Dan's request. By honoring her word she betrays his family; by breaking her word she betrays Dan. There was no good reason to put herself in that position in the first place. Once having made that error, it would only make things worse by sticking to it.

# 8

# Should I Stop Someone from Hurting Himself?

Carolyn's recently widowed father, Sam, is depressed. He refuses to eat properly. He tells Carolyn that the doctor reports that he has extremely high blood pressure and is in danger of having a stroke. He will not listen to his daughter, and he ignores his doctor's advice to change his eating habits and remove salt from his diet.

One day, while her father is out, Carolyn goes to his apartment and removes all packaged and canned foods containing salt. In their place she leaves foods better suited for a person suffering from hypertension.

Some questions to ask yourself:

1. Under what circumstances should adults not be allowed to make choices for themselves?
2. Who should decide if a person is incapable of taking care of himself?
3. Should a person be allowed to determine the quality of life he desires?
4. How do you decide between a rational decision that you

disagree with, and an irrational decision that may not be the best for another person?

5. How do you know what is best?
6. Is it possible to respect a person and disregard his wishes?
7. Is it possible to respect a person and not take into account what he may want for himself if he understood the complete picture?
8. Do you approve of Carolyn's actions?

# The Problem:
## Adult in Years versus Adult in Judgment

Parents are held liable for neglecting the well-being of their children, but the law doesn't hold people accountable for the well-being of other adults in the same way. The arguments for interfering in the life of a child who is thought to be suicidal can be compelling, since we believe that children are not fully competent to make potentially life-altering decisions for themselves. That's why voting is reserved for people above a certain age. But when it comes to interfering in the life of an adult who may be headed down a path of self-destruction, the reasons for invading someone's privacy are less clear. That's why hospitals can't require patients to stay against their will. Respect for a person requires granting the right to self-determination, even if others think someone is making a serious mistake.

The exception to this general rule of self-determination is when a person is not mentally competent. But modern medicine has created some new problems as people are living longer.

The upshot of extending longevity is that adult children often are forced into acting like parents to their own parents. So the question of paternalism is turned on its head. Instead of parents taking care of children, children now have to take care of their parents.

# Depression and Impaired Judgment

Milagros Sanchez, a rehabilitation counselor who has worked in California and Florida, says that the story presented here is fairly common. I asked her what she thought was going on. "Depression," she says. "The greatest challenge facing disabled adults is generally not the physical challenges but rather the emotional ones. Depression is the greatest debilitation for all injured or ill persons. It prevents them from taking full advantage of all the wonderful scientific and human resources available to them. Often they sabotage their recovery efforts."

A depressed person isn't merely sad or listless. Such a person really can't think clearly, as the weight of the world seems to descend upon the body and the mind. Everything is viewed through a glass darkly. There is no sense of the future, except one with more of the same despair or worse.

There's a difference between a teenager being depressed and an old man being depressed. A teenager does have his future before him, but an old person, under the best of circumstances, doesn't have much of a future to look forward to. If at all possible, we want to treat the young person so he can experience life fully. The situation with the elderly is somewhat different. Maybe his loss is so great that the future can only bring him continued pain, even if he weren't depressed. Maybe Sam should be allowed the right to his own sadness. Sailfish, for example, mate for life, and when one dies the other surfaces to die also. Without their lifelong companion, their life becomes empty. I don't know what meaning Sam's marriage had for him, but it is conceivable that he finds no purpose in living any longer. In a time in which everything seems disposable and substitutable, I find nobility in the person whose grief at the death of a longtime spouse is so great that his life is not worth living. In our society, with such an emphasis upon youth and entertainment, many believe that everyone has not only the right to be happy, but the duty. However, Sanchez points out that healing from the loss of a beloved spouse can take a long time. "Clearly, Carolyn's father has not had enough time as yet to grieve and get beyond his loss," she says.

Sanchez continues, "Many of us with good moral and ethical intentions are quick to solve others' problems for them. But it is Sam who must face his emotional challenges, overcome his depression, and go on with his life. It is he who is responsible for his health, for whether he continues to live or die. He may not have the tools with which to better cope with his loss, depression, and illness. He may simply need more time to adjust to his circumstances. Without question, he is in need of loving support."

## Taking Charge

There are two major questions in this situation: Should Carolyn step in and take over for her father, and assuming that she should do something, what is it that she should do?

Not everyone agrees that Carolyn has an obligation to look out for her father's welfare. One popular idea is that people are responsible only for themselves. This is a useful principle. It prevents us from becoming busybodies and it provides a basis for being tolerant. If people would simply stop telling others how to act, then we'd all be a bit happier for it. Also, if I am responsible only for myself, it means that no one else is responsible for me. So I become more independent and less likely to see myself as a victim. But the principle has its limitations. The wall between me and others can be too high, resulting in loneliness. It also can make me mean-spirited in the sense that I view other people's failures as always being their own fault. Self-determination isn't a community builder or a road to a compassionate world.

This is especially true when it comes to intimate relationships.

Family life demands more than personal responsibility. It means being drawn into another's life. Caring about another person requires that we do things to help, even when the helping is difficult, even, sometimes, when our help isn't wanted. Family ties are often tangles and knots. I have always found George Eliot's aphorism appealing: "What are you here for if not to make life easier for one another?" That seems right to me. As someone who has had training as a marital therapist and works as a clergyman, I have heard and seen the intimate, sad stories of family lives. I know full well the ways in which families become nests of destruction, the unhappiness that families can sow. But separateness and distance are lousy alternatives. People die from alienation as well as repression.

Carolyn is faced with what appear to be life-and-death decisions about her father. So an attitude of not caring is hardly an acceptable ethical stance. The question remains, though, what should she do? *How* to get Sam to change his eating habits is the problem, not whether it is *right* to get him to change. The correctness of Carolyn's aim isn't the question, but the method of achieving it is.

## Emotional Support

Sanchez gives some practical advice. "Carolyn clearly loves her father, and it is that love which drives her to take action, but her vision is shortsighted. Removing the foods harmful to her father is a short-term solution. It is better to stop, think, and ask why. Why is Dad not willing to take care of his health? What is he feeling? How can I be supportive of him so that he will feel better? It is critical to not become an enabler but rather help those in need to help themselves. It is through those types of efforts that you can truly make a significant difference in others' lives. The most difficult choice sometimes is the choice to not become an enabler. I think this is particularly difficult for women, who are often cast in the role of caretakers."

Sanchez continues, "The best steps Carolyn could take would be to spend quality time with her father and support him emotionally as he deals with his loss and struggles with his depression. She can listen to him. She can involve him in her activities as much as possible. She can encourage him to seek counseling for his depression. She can research supportive and educational resources available in his community and offer to go with him. She can educate herself on depression and loss and thus be better able to find real solutions to her father's problem."

## Emergency Steps

Sanchez may well be right about the practical steps for Carolyn. But what if it takes weeks or maybe months to become effective? Meanwhile, the doctor is afraid that Sam is in immediate danger of a stroke.

If someone is elderly and at risk, there may be only short-term solutions. The ultimate goal is to get Sam through his depression so that he can find a fruitful life once more. The methods suggested by Sanchez may not work quickly enough. If in Carolyn's assessment, based upon the doctor's best judgment, going into Sam's apartment without his permission to change some cans of food will help him to live the life that he truly desires, then her action is not such a bad thing to do and can be morally justified.

As with other situations that are exceptions to the rule, there is the danger that the exception becomes the rule. Carolyn's action should be seen as an emergency step. She needs as quickly as possible to return to a position where her father is in control of his own life. His sense of dignity needs to be protected by him being granted the right to self-determination.

# 9

# What Does Personal Loyalty Require of Me?

Curtis comes from a small-farm family. He wants to be a doctor but can't afford a top school. However, he gets an appointment to a military academy where he will get an excellent education, tuition-free. The academy has an honor system. Anyone caught cheating will be expelled. The code also requires that cadets report anyone they suspect of cheating. Curtis discovers that his roommate and friend, Ted, whom he has known since childhood, has submitted a partially plagiarized term paper. Curtis cannot convince Ted to admit the infraction to school authorities. According to the academy's rules, Curtis must now report his friend. However, he refuses to do this. He resigns from the academy instead.

Some questions to ask yourself:

1. Does Curtis's background make a difference in how you judge his decision?
2. How important a part should Curtis's career goals play?
3. Do you think that Curtis's loyalty should be foremost to his friend or the military?

4. What does Curtis owe his friend?
5. What does Curtis owe himself?
6. Under what circumstances do you think it is right for someone to jeopardize his own future?
7. Do you think that Curtis is upholding the honor system or
   violating it?
8. Do you think Curtis is doing the moral thing by leaving the
   academy?

# The Problem:
## Integrity versus Personal Success

This is an ethically difficult issue. It isn't a choice between two
conflicting values but three—taking care of oneself, playing by
the rules, and loyalty to a friend

Curtis has his own life to lead. Curtis, as a young man, has
properly set himself on a course to achieve certain life goals.
What's more, most of us would agree that he has chosen an
admirable career. He wants to help people, and that, by definition, is a good thing. Self-care is an important component in
ethics. Without caring about ourselves, we couldn't be compassionate, for it doesn't make sense to care about others but not care
about ourselves. Compassion requires that we feel what others
feel. If we can't feel for ourselves, we can't feel adequately for
others, either.

Curtis is a decent person who wants to abide by the rules. It
wouldn't be right to take the scholarship from the academy, then
turn around and disregard the code that he agreed to follow.
Whether he agrees with the honor code is beside the point. He
knew what he was getting into, he did it voluntarily, and he feels
duty bound to follow its dictates. He doesn't stray from the rule
as it applies to himself. The difficulty is that it is someone else

who has broken the rule, which requires him to do something that violates his conscience.

Curtis feels bound not only by the military's written rule but also by the unwritten rules of friendship. He has a keen sense of loyalty to those who are close to him. Despite his efforts to get Ted to take action, his friend refuses. Then Curtis is faced with breaking either the academy's honor code or his own. He could save his own career by turning in his friend, or protect his friend and ruin his own career.

## The Need for Military Officers to Have Good Character

Stephen Arata is a lieutenant colonel who has had a command position in Germany, Panama, and Haiti and as the U.S. liaison officer to the French War College. He is currently an assistant professor of history at West Point. During Arata's first year at West Point, one of the worst cheating scandals in the academy's history rocked the institution. "As a young plebe [freshman] I had to watch as day after day, cadets that I had grown to respect and trust were brought before honor boards, found guilty, forced to clear their rooms, and then dismissed from the academy. Most of these cadets were found guilty and dismissed because of toleration. At the end of it all, almost one-third of the West Point class of 1977 had been expelled from the academy."

Arata witnessed the consequences of the honor code as it is used by the military, and he supports it fully. I also support it, but with a reservation.

Arata and I share a number of concerns. We both believe that the academy's job is to make the best officers possible. They must become skillful commanders of warriors. Also, we both believe that good character is essential for good officers.

Arata and I agree that there is good reason to have an honor code. There is no place for commanders who lie, cheat, or steal.

## Getting What You Want

When I present this problem to students of mine, almost all think that Curtis should turn in Ted. They say that if Ted were really a friend of Curtis's, he wouldn't have put him in that position in the first place.

"But he did," I say. "This is what really happened. You can't wish for Ted to do something else. He may regret it later, but at this time Curtis is stuck with the situation."

In that case, Curtis should report Ted, most students tell me. But their reasons seldom have to do with supporting the honor code or obeying rules. Typically, they say something like this: "Curtis should not have sacrificed his educational opportunities because of the dishonesty of another student, no matter what principle was involved. I believe that if you want something, nobody should stand in your way of achieving it."

## To Follow or Not to Follow Orders?

Another reason typically given is that Curtis knew the rules when he entered the academy and therefore he had to abide by them. There's a rule and it's wrong to violate it. The line of reasoning has it limitations, though. While the military wants soldiers who follow orders, it doesn't want people to follow orders blindly. Orders have to be orders that don't violate universal codes of conduct.

This point was made when three U.S. soldiers were given the Soldier's Medal, the highest award for bravery not involving conflict with the enemy. Hugh Thompson, Lawrence Colburn, and Glen Andreotta happened upon the My Lai massacre when they landed their helicopter in the line of fire between U.S. troops and fleeing Vietnamese civilians. They pointed their guns at American soldiers to prevent the further massacre of civilians, and Thompson, while under cover by Colburn and Andreotta, confronted the leader of the American forces.

In awarding the medals, Major General Michael Ackerman said, "It was their ability to do the right thing even at the risk of their personal safety that guided these soldiers to do what they did." That the soldiers did not receive this honor until thirty years after the fact underscores how highly the military values following orders.

Another important value in the military is loyalty to other soldiers. Arata says, "Most young men and women accepted at an academy have excelled as team players for a long time. They are experts at trying to minimize a teammate's weakness. They have worked hard to build esprit and confidence among their peers. At an academy, many students have difficulty accepting the 'toleration' clause of the honor code because it flies in he face of being a good team player. Turning someone in for lying, cheating, or stealing means instant dismissal for the guilty party—a heavy price to pay.

"I prayed that I would never have to make that decision," Arata says. "West Point cadets will always struggle with the question of toleration, as I did when I was a young cadet in the summer of 1975. But in the end, each cadet will conclude that the honor code is essential and timeless. Its strictures are critical to the survival of our military and the character of our officer corps."

When cadets enter the academy, they know the rules. No cheating. No condoning of cheating. No cover-ups. Ted has violated the rule, and Curtis would violate it, too, if he doesn't report him. At the point Curtis knows what Ted has done, he faces several choices: do nothing and thereby become complicit, turn in his friend, or resign. He chooses the last course, presumably at great cost to himself. After all, he accepted the appointment to the academy not because he necessarily wants a military life but because he wants to become a doctor and the academy offered that possibility.

## Honor and Loyalty

The first alternative—doing and saying nothing—isn't a real choice for him. He believes that he has a duty to live by the guidelines laid down by the academy for all its cadets. As long as he remains in the school, he feels bound by them. In military terms, he has a direct order: report all cheating.

The second choice—reporting Ted—means betraying a friendship. Because he has failed to persuade Ted to report himself, as the honor code requires, it now is incumbent upon Curtis to carry out his part of the bargain. But how can he squeal on his friend? Friends are supposed stand by one another, be loyal to each other, protect, sacrifice, and support one another. One soldier is supposed to give his life for another, if need be. So if Curtis reports Ted's plagiarism, it can hardly be called an act of friendship, except in the way a parent punishes a child and claims, "This hurts me more than it hurts you." Maybe it will be good for Ted in the long run that he live with the consequences of his actions, but who is Curtis to make that decision about his friend's life?

If Curtis reports Ted, Ted will be thrown out of the academy. If Curtis says nothing and Ted says nothing, Ted remains a cadet. Of course, in a real sense Ted would be the person responsible for his own expulsion, since he knowingly violated the school's rule. But in the immediate sense, Curtis would be the cause of Ted being discharged from the academy. If the school doesn't know about the plagiarism, then it as much as didn't happen—like a tree not really falling in a forest if no one heard it crash.

Ted is less than honorable for cheating; he is less than honorable for not turning himself in; and he is less than honorable for putting Curtis in such an awful spot. But if Curtis reports Ted, he will hurt a friend. In all likelihood, once the academy knows about Ted's violation, it will expel him. Clearly, Ted would be hurt by this. There would be a permanent mark against him. While people do overcome such things and may even become better people because of it, there is no guarantee that Ted would benefit. He could just as easily become despondent and wreck the rest of his life.

Is it any of Curtis's concern what happens to Ted? Certainly. Friends care about what happens to each other. Of course, one might ask what kind of friend is Ted to put Curtis in such a spot in the first place. Nevertheless, he did and now Curtis has to deal with it. He can't will it away or wish that Ted were other than the person he is. It is because he is his friend, because he cares about what happens to him, because he wants the best for him that Curtis has a serious dilemma. Precisely because Curtis is Ted's friend, he has such loyalty to him.

But Curtis has another other loyalty as well. He is devoted to the academy and its standard of honesty. He isn't protesting the honor code system, nor is he critical of the academy in general. I assume that he would stay in school, all other things being equal. By trying to persuade Ted to report himself, it seems clear that he favors the rules as they are—or at least thinks that cadets ought to abide by them until they are changed. While Ted may not want to live by the code (or perhaps does but is too weak to overcome the temptation to cheat in order to get a better grade), Curtis wants to live by the rules.

# The Importance of Friendship

Given the conflicting demands of friendship and an honor code, Curtis finds another way out. He leaves. This isn't the coward's choice. Rather, Curtis's decision is made at great personal sacrifice. He gives up his chance to graduate from his school of choice and thereby jeopardizes his own future.

Is this too much to give to a friend who is the one at fault? I don't think so. It seems to me to be an admirable thing to do, an act of great courage. He is going beyond what duty to the school requires of him and what Ted can fairly expect of him. In making his decision, Curtis is choosing a set of values more important than his own material gain. More important than being an academy graduate, Curtis is choosing friendship. And more important than being a dishonest student by breaking the honor code, he is choosing his own integrity.

What makes this vignette morally ambiguous is that Ted isn't an innocent victim and that Curtis sacrifices his place at the academy for someone who himself should resign. Ted shouldn't force this choice upon his friend Curtis, who here really is the innocent victim. Curtis, then, is penalized for something not of his own making. But such is the situation, and the decision then has become Curtis's to make.

In an ideal world, Ted wouldn't have plagiarized the paper; in a slightly less than ideal world, Ted would report himself. But in this story, as is often the case, the world is less than ideal. People exhibit weakness, do regrettable things, and inadvertently impose their problems upon others. The question is, what is the right thing to do in this less than perfect world?

If Curtis were to report Ted, this too, it could be argued, is the right thing to do. Many of my students take this tack. They say that Ted, after all, would only be getting what he deserves. But there is a more sophisticated reason to be offered, and it is made by Arata, who says, "Curtis did the wrong thing by resigning because he did not fully understand the true meaning of, and need for, honor in the military. The military is a team that deals in solders', sailors', and airmen's lives, not wins or losses. In the military, confidence in one's superiors, subordinates, and peers has literally meant the difference between life and death. History is replete with examples of soldiers who risked their lives defending a position because of their confidence in their leaders, their fellow soldiers in the line with them, and their support troops who have promised them as much artillery, air and ammunition support as they need. Americans have won from Yorktown to Iraq because of this confidence."

## Self-Sacrifice as a Military Value

Arata's points are good ones. If Curtis reports Ted instead of resigning, I wouldn't judge his actions as morally wrong. But Curtis chooses another course. And since Curtis is willing to sacrifice his own interests for the sake of their friendship, I have to assume that he isn't acting impulsively. He must have given it careful thought and agonized over the decision. He knows Ted well, he understands the terms under which he accepted the appointment, he knows the consequences for himself by choosing what he does. Still he does it. Maybe he knows something about Ted. Perhaps he sees that Ted's infraction was minor; perhaps he sees this as a once-in-a-lifetime lapse and that Ted will learn from his moment of weakness and that he will still be a good military leader.

Arata reaches the opposite conclusion. He thinks that Curtis could never have confidence again in Ted, and that the military must be built on the absolute trust and confidence in its officers.

So Arata and I differ. I think that given these various considerations, Curtis has taken the higher road by taking on someone else's burden, and for this he deserves high praise. His actions go beyond the call of duty; they are supererogatory. Perhaps it is more than can be expected of the ordinary person, to take loyalty to this height, but I view it as a model of ethical behavior. I am reminded of E. M. Forster's comment "If I had to choose between betraying my country and betraying my friend, I hope I should have the guts to betray my country."

## Breaking the Rule for a Higher Value

This is a real story. I know Curtis (a pseudonym), so I am familiar with how events actually unfolded.

After leaving the military academy, Curtis spent a year in a state university. He then received a telephone call from West Point. The authorities there hadn't understood why he had resigned, but now they knew. Ted had finally confessed to his cheating. Curtis was invited to return to the academy. He accepted and went on to complete his education there.

I suppose the military believed that loyalty to one's comrades and the willingness to engage in self-sacrifice outweighed the violation of the rules. Since Curtis couldn't live up to all three virtues esteemed by the military—following orders, loyalty, and self-sacrifice—fulfilling two out of three was enough for the academy to readmit him.

Curtis is now chief of medicine at one the military's leading hospitals. He is also chair of its ethics committee.

# 10

❦

# Is It Right for Me to Use Someone to Make My Point?

Charlotte is twelve. Her brother, Roland, is nine. Their father, Fred, discovers that they stole five dollars from his wallet to buy candy and play video games. He scolds them both but penalizes only Charlotte, claiming that as the older of the two she should have known better. He wants to make an example of her so that Roland won't ever steal again.

Some questions to ask yourself:

1. Should the same penalty for the same infraction apply to everyone?
2. Is the purpose of punishment to cause enough (material) pain so the offender will be too afraid do it again?
3. Do you punish someone because no one should get away with doing something wrong?
4. If the purpose of punishment is to prevent future harm, what if anything is the problem with using an example of what could happen to someone who has done wrong?

5. How old should someone be before you hold her accountable for what she's done?
6. Is Fred acting ethically?

# The Problem:
## Punishing the Wrongdoer or
## Punishing to Prevent Future Harm?

What you think of how Fred punishes his children depends on
your philosophy of punishment in general and what you think is
the best way to raise children in particular.

Let's look at the philosophy part first. A common view is that
if someone has done something wrong, he should make good.
Exodus 22:1 states, "If a man steal an ox, or a sheep and kill it, or
sell it; he shall restore five oxen for an ox, and four sheep for a
sheep." We also assume that the person who is punished should
be the person who has done the wrong. Deuteronomy 24:16
states the principle this way: "The father shall not be put to death
for the children, neither shall the children be put to death for the
fathers: every man shall be put to death for his own sin."

Most of us support this ethical principle, but there are some
who disagree. In fact, punishing the innocent for the crimes of
their ancestors was an ancient practice. The Passover story is an
especially vivid example, as the Egyptian children are killed because
of the acts of the Pharaoh. And in biblical times, the scapegoat
was an animal sacrificed for the sins of people.

But we don't have go back two thousand years to find people
who punish not the guilty party but others who stand in their
place. In a small section of western Africa, there is a tradition in
which a young girl can be made a virtual sex slave to a priest of
the local religion for crimes committed by her ancestors. The
trokosi is a wife of the gods and serves an indefinite period of

servitude, until the priest is satisfied that the guilt of the past crime has been expiated. Another example is Israel's destruction of the homes of civilian Palestinians in retaliation for assaults by other Palestinians.

These practices are wholly unacceptable from an ethical point of view, because they violate a central ethical principle, namely, respect for the individual person. This means that we can't use people as a means to an end only. People should get what they deserve, neither unfairly benefiting from someone else's actions or suffering because of what someone did. So we should punish those who deserve it and not inflict punishment upon those who don't. This principle explains one of the rules of war: civilians can't be targets, nor can civilians be used as shields by soldiers.

## Punishment: Making It Fit the Crime

Related to this concept is the idea that the punishment should fit the crime. At its most basic level it is an "an eye for an eye, a tooth for a tooth," a concept found in Mosaic, Roman, and other ancient laws. The basic point of *lex talionis* is that if the crime is small, so should be the penalty, and if the crime is serious, the penalty should be equally severe. In other words, the extent of the punishment should be proportionate to the wrongdoing. This is why you have different sentences for the severity of the crimes. Who wouldn't be bothered by a driver getting a fifty-year sentence for going through a red light while a mass murderer walks away with only a fine? Everyone understands that the police may have to use force to stop a criminal assault, but we are less willing to justify the use of deadly force to stop a petty offense. This is the principle of proportionality, one of the factors in the Catholic calculation of a just war.

The principle of just punishment is used as a defense of the death penalty for heinous crimes. The principled ethical argument in favor of the death penalty runs like this: Nothing is worse than deliberately and gratuitously taking another's life, and therefore, the punishment should be as severe as the crime itself. The dead cannot be brought back to life, but society can express its moral outrage by exacting the most severe penalty in return, namely, taking the life of the murderer. This isn't revenge exactly. It is more like righting the scales. Likewise, there are compelling ethical arguments to oppose the death penalty, such as not imitating the worst behavior of the person whom you intend to punish, or not legitimizing violence as a whole by state killing. If all we wanted to do was to exact the worst possible punishment, we wouldn't execute people behind closed doors but on Main Street. And we wouldn't be looking for humane methods of execution, but would find the most horrible forms of torture possible.

Good people can be found on both sides of the capital punishment debate. However, the point I am making here is one that both sides agree upon. Terrible crimes require severe punishment.

## Punishment as a Deterrent

There is yet another moral argument for the death penalty. Capital punishment, it is claimed, serves as a deterrent. It surely prevents future crime, because the perpetrator can't commit any more acts of any kind since he is now dead. This argument is on less certain moral grounds than the ones presented before. Let's assume that there is evidence that state executions in fact lower the violent crime rate (a much debated theory). Is this a strong enough moral argument to execute people? If the point of punishment is to lower crime rates, then it really doesn't even matter if the right person is being punished. As long as the punishment scares enough people so they don't commit murder themselves, authorities may as well make a spectacle of whoever happens to be handy. This isn't morally acceptable.

So, going back to our example, if Charlotte's father punishes her simply to make a point with Roland, he is on weak moral ground, even if it keeps Roland on the straight and narrow.

# Responsibility:
## It Requires the Ability to Know That What You Are Doing Is Wrong

People are punished if they have done something wrong, but not if they couldn't have done otherwise. We don't hold someone responsible if he has acted under duress. If a person steals money because someone else held a gun to his head, the person isn't a thief. Morality has meaning only for those who have free will, that is, those who when faced with a decision are capable of freely choosing one thing or another.

People also aren't culpable if they can't understand the difference between right and wrong. The mentally incompetent aren't liable for their actions. And this is why, given what we know about the nature of other creatures, moral responsibility applies only to human beings. This wasn't always the case. In France during the Middle Ages, for example, a horse that had kicked a farrier to death was tried for murder. Even inanimate objects weren't spared. A trial was held for a church bell that had fallen on the head of the ringer, causing his death. The bell faced the ignominious fate of being smelted. These examples seem bizarre, because today the difference between intent and accident appears obvious. There aren't trials for fallen objects, but there are trials for the person who may have caused the object to fall in the first place.

When you move on to why someone does something and their mental capacity to understand, you are leaving the area of philosophy and moving into that of psychology. Philosophy tells us that only those who have free will can be held liable for what they do. Psychology tells us that bells aren't liable for the damage they cause because bells can't reason and therefore have no free will. Responsibility requires some intelligence and/or mental competence. Therefore, a person may have committed a crime but can be found not guilty as a result of insanity or mental deficiency. A lunatic who commits a crime is criminally insane, and therefore is considered more a psychiatric patient than a criminal. And a person with a very low IQ who commits a crime may be institutionalized to prevent future harm, but she doesn't otherwise get punished for her crime. Similarly, when a three-year-old smothers another child to death, it is a great tragedy but no crime.

## The Age Factor:
## Young Children Aren't Fully Responsible

Harmful acts done by young children are accidents. Five-year-olds, no matter what harm they may have done, aren't imprisoned. But the older someone is, the more difficult it becomes to decide how guilty to hold him. Do we jail ten-year-olds? No? What about sixteen-year-olds? The United Nations had to consider exactly this in the aftermath of the civil war in Sierra Leone. Children as young as fifteen participated in mass slaughters of civilians. Should they be tried and sentenced as adults? The UN legal department decided that fifteen- to eighteen-year-olds, if found guilty, should be sent to rehabilitation centers rather than to prisons. Fourteen-year-olds can go to prison in Massachusetts, twelve-year-olds in Oregon, and in Wisconsin one only needs to be ten. At eighteen no one has a doubt—we can vote, we can go to prison. The point is that age and mental competence are mitigating factors. Where to draw the line is not easy to know, and legally, such distinctions vary from place to place and from time to time. Yet we can all agree at the extremes. Two-year-olds, no; twenty-year-olds, yes.

But in our example, Charlotte and Roland are only three years apart. Perhaps they are at the same developmental level, but this is not likely. If they are typical for their age, Charlotte is more sophisticated in her understanding than Roland. In addition, Charlotte's offense is probably greater because, as the older sister, she should have known better. If, in fact, she was the instigator or didn't try to stop her younger brother or egged him on, then she has a greater degree of responsibility and therefore deserves a greater punishment. Children are rightly given more responsibilities as they grow older. Along with this comes greater accountability.

At nine years old, Roland understands that stealing is wrong. Therefore, he should be punished for what he has done. At twelve years old, Charlotte has a better grasp of why stealing is wrong. So it is also right that her punishment be a little more severe than her brother's. However, Fred's decision not to punish Roland at all, and to punish Charlotte not for her sake alone but to make an example out of her, is morally unacceptable.

## A Proper Punishment: What Will Happen?

My response so far has been at the level of philosophy and psychology. So I asked Ellen McBride what she thought about this situation. As a lawyer who sits as a small claims arbitrator, she sees people who are often in the midst of minor but bitter disputes and so brings to this situation a more practical turn of mind. McBride says, "The question first to be asked is why the money was stolen by the two children. I ask these questions regardless of their ages: One, were candy and video games prohibited by the father and therefore the children were not given money for these endeavors? Two, did the children previously ask the father for money to buy candy and video games, and were they denied? Three, is there a family policy against these diversions? Four, are they budgeted for within the family? Five, did the children steal the money because their friends put pressure on them to do or have things forbidden to them? Six, was this just a mischievous prank?"

McBride had another set of questions. "Knowing more about the two children would also be helpful. You might ask: One, was either child under a disability that would render that child incapable of knowing right from wrong? Two, does the relationship of the two children encompass the greater influence of one over the other? Three, were there other peer pressures involved? Four, was either child angry with the father? Why?"

McBride is concerned as much with what is going to happen later as she is with meting out proper punishment. "The example setting is to my mind most ineffective here because Roland was already involved in the act and at nine (if under no disability) is quite capable of knowing that he got off without punishment and that Charlotte is being punished. An explanation of differences in ages is not enough. It says to Roland, 'When you are twelve I expect that you will know that stealing is not right or acceptable behavior but at nine you are less responsible for your actions.' Roland could easily take this as license to steal until he turns twelve. Charlotte on the other hand might well have taken this as unjust punishment. One of the worst elements of the uneven penalty is the setting of one sibling against another. In all circumstances where I have seen this done, it never fails to work either as a bond between the siblings if they are more sensitive to the injustice or as a cause for a rift between them."

# A Moral Mistake:
# Using a Person as a Means Only

McBride is probably right. But I don't know for sure what Roland and Charlotte will learn from this. I don't know how it will affect their relationship with each other or with their father. Probably it won't be good, but it's conceivable that it might work out for the best. Whether the father's punishment will, in fact, lead to a good or bad outcome depends upon context and family history, something that can be known only by those who are intimate with the family. It's enough for me to say that Fred is wrong because it is morally unacceptable to use a person to make a point with someone else.

Immanuel Kant said that to respect a person means that we can't use him as a means only. Of course, we use people all the time—the checkout person at the counter, the conductor on the bus, and so forth. We don't have a relationship with those people except insofar as we use them for something we want. Even so, we must respect them as people, just as we hope they won't be rude to us. Kant meant that there is no justification for merely using someone as if he were a thing. This is what Fred is doing by using his daughter as an example to make a point with his son. This is using Charlotte as a means only, and so it is unethical.

## 11

✖

# Is Life Always
# Worth Living?

Moe and Anne have been married for more than sixty years. Anne is beginning to suffer from Alzheimer's disease: she asks the same question several times, writes on the bottom of plates, and does other strange things. While she continues to do household chores, such as cooking and cleaning, she has also lost the ability to make sound judgments. Moe decides everything for both of them. While close to ninety, Moe is still active.

Anne has begun to suffer heart problems, and the doctor tells Moe that Anne needs surgery to prevent what in all likelihood will be a serious heart attack within the year. He also assures Moe that the surgery required is nearly routine and has a very high success rate, even in a woman of Anne's advanced age.

"But," the surgeon asks, "at your age, will you be able to care for her? She'll have a healthy body but her mind is going rapidly. She may well live for another five to ten years if she has the operation."

Moe has to decide for his wife whether to go ahead with the procedure.

Some questions to ask yourself:

1. Is withholding a lifesaving procedure the same as killing someone?
2. Who should make the decisions about the health of another person when that person cannot make it for herself?
3. Is it uncaring to let a person die?
4. Is it selfish to prolong someone's life because you don't want to be without her?
5. What do you think Moe should do?

# The Problem:
# One Person's Life versus
# Another's Quality of Life

I know this problem better than any other in the book. Anne and Moe were my parents. My father was put into the position of having to choose life or death for his longtime wife. For some this isn't a problem at all. They don't have to think about it, they won't agonize over the decision, as there will be no decision to be made. They will always choose life, no matter how bleak the prospects may be for all concerned. If there is a chance that surgery will prolong life, they will take it. If there is hope that some treatment will help, no matter how experimental or unproven, they will opt for it. If a person can live only as long as they are tethered to a machine, they will keep the person hooked up. They will not let someone die no matter what, and they will do everything in their power to keep a person alive.

My father didn't have such assurances. He had a decision to make—whether to keep my mother alive or let her die. He had to decide what the quality of her life would be like if she lived. He had to decide what the quality of his life would be like if he let her die.

I didn't know my mother had Alzheimer's until I flew down to Florida to be with my parents because my mother had had a minor heart attack. My father had never mentioned my mother's dementia before, nor had my brother, who lived not far from our parents. When we had spoken on the phone, my mother always sounded fine. She was more forgetful, but still she carried on simple conversations and told me about the weather and such. It wasn't so different from conversations in the past. But now when I spent time with her, I realized that she wasn't right. My father said that it had happened suddenly. It wasn't the usual forgetfulness of not remembering where she put the keys, but something far more serious.

My father was in his mid-eighties at that time. He was in excellent health and very vigorous. But I wondered what my father would do if my mother died or if he had to take care of her. He had never lived alone in his life, not even when he was a bachelor. My mother took care of all the household chores. My father had never cooked, washed dishes, cleaned, made beds, or done laundry.

My brother and I went to the doctor's office with my father when he was presented with the situation. The surgeon said that at the rate at which my mother's mental state was deteriorating, which my father agreed was rapid, she wouldn't be able to care for herself within a year or so. There were two options. The first was to let nature take its course and not operate. Then, in all probability, she would die from heart disease within the year. The second course was do the operation. The surgeon explained that it was a relatively low-risk procedure, one that he had been doing for more than twenty years with 100 percent success, and Anne would essentially have a healthy, normal heart.

My father would then have to care for my mother. If she continued to mentally deteriorate at the rate of the last few months, her mental faculties would be all but gone in a short time. My father then would be faced with two other choices: care for her himself or institutionalize her.

My father wavered wildly, one minute saying that my mother would have no quality of life with Alzheimer's disease, the next saying that it would be like killing her if he didn't consent to the operation.

## Understanding the Disease

What are the facts about Alzheimer's? I wondered. My father needed to make his decision immediately, so we had to rely upon what he said and upon our own knowledge of the disease. But afterward I did ask one of the country's leading Alzheimer's researchers, psychiatrist Steven Targum. He said, "Moe's dilemma is a common scenario in the lives of many elderly couples. The incidence of Alzheimer's disease exceeds 20 percent in adults over the age of eighty, who frequently have comorbid medical conditions like heart disease as well. Alzheimer's is a gradual disease, which progresses at different rates based upon genetics, nutrition, other medical problems, and luck."

What did he think Moe should have done? Targum couldn't say without knowing more facts. "Moe may believe that the inevitable loss of mental and physical capacity associated with the progressive deterioration of Alzheimer's disease is unacceptable and that a death from 'natural' causes is more dignified for his wife.

"Alternatively, Moe would not be the first man to care for a demented wife until she needed nursing home placement. The decision to provide life-sustaining surgery for Anne requires consideration of social, emotional, and financial issues, which extend beyond the mere event of the surgery. It is not unusual for a surviving spouse to fail physically and emotionally shortly after the loss of their lifelong partner."

Targum continued, "It is possible that the grieving process that is considered to be normal and healthy may be insurmountable in a ninety-year-old man who has sustained himself on a sixty-year relationship. Ultimately, the decision to consent to life-sustaining surgery for Anne depends upon Moe's perspective on the meaning of their relationship and his ability to care for her financially, physically, and emotionally without succumbing himself."

## Understanding One's Feelings

I also wondered what a therapist thought about my father and the decision he faced. So I asked Carol Targum, Steven's wife, a social worker specializing in family matters. She said, "I am concerned with the quality of the interactions between the couple and the impact on their relationship. Anne has lost her ability to use sound judgment and decision making. Although the surgery will repair her body, it cannot repair her mind. The mutual reciprocity that characterizes most long-term marriages has begun to decline and would continue to do so."

She then asked a series of questions to help to clarify the emotional facts. "What are Moe's reactions to his wife's illness? Does he feel stress both physically and emotionally from providing constant care for a chronic illness, or would this care be the culmination of lifelong loving and nurturing? What type of support system does he have among family and friends? What additional burden does this place upon their modest financial means?" Targum continued, "Old age is a time of loss. Issues of dependency surface which can create their own set of anxieties centered around feelings of helplessness, anger, and guilt for being healthy and still alive. It raises issues about self-worth—am I a good person if I do or do not let this happen? How selfish can I be? What do I owe myself and what do I owe my wife in these circumstances? From my perspective, quality of life becomes the critical factor. Anne's continued impaired functioning coupled with Moe's increased caretaking responsibilities necessitate a reevaluation of their relationship. What is the quality of their life together? What is the quality of life for each of the individuals? Allowing nature to take its course can be a loving gesture that preserves the dignity of both partners."

## Feeling Guilty

My brother and I weren't able to think this clearly under the circumstances. But my father did want to know what we thought he should do. He was using us as a way to think out loud. He didn't want to be told what to do, but our thoughts were important to him. He knew the responsibility was completely his own. There were the practical matters to think through, but there was also another, separate element. He was seeking moral guidance, for he truly didn't know what was the right choice and he had to choose between unhappy alternatives.

"If I can save her, I have to do it," he would say one moment. "I have the power to save her life. If I don't choose that, it's like I've killed her." He would be silent for a while. Then he would say, "But she's going to become a person without a mind. She never wanted to live where she can't take care of herself. I won't be able to take care of her for long before she'll have to go to an institution. She said she never wanted that. She couldn't stand to even visit friends who were in nursing homes." He continued to carry on this debate with himself. Whenever he seemed to firmly decide on one course of action, I said I agreed with him, even if I had reservations. He needed my support in whatever choice he made. But a short while later he would change his mind, and once again, I would agree with his decision, even though it contradicted the earlier one.

I don't think I was much help in assisting my father to make his decision, except perhaps as a sounding board. But my brother and I were useful in letting him know that the choices were impossible and that whichever decision he made would be the right one.

Even before my mother became ill, I had thought about the social problems caused by people living longer. I didn't raise these with my father. That would have been inappropriate, cruel even, at the time. But it was in the back of my mind.

Given the fact that any society has limited funds and has to make choices about how to spend its money, there is a policy issue here. Society needs to consider the interests of everyone involved and to consider those interests disinterestedly. According to the National Institute on Aging/National Institutes of Health, the cost of caring for one person with severe cognitive impairments at home or at a nursing home is more than $47,000 per year. "The annual economic toll of Alzheimer's disease in the United States in terms of health care expenses and lost wages of both patients and their caregivers is estimated at $80 to $100 billion."

Perhaps society should be spending such a staggering sum on its children instead of its elderly. This is a public policy question that rests upon ethical considerations—the fairest way of redistributing society's resources. We never talked about this when my father was making his decision, because this wasn't any woman but *my* mother, *my* father's wife. It was right that we focused only on her at that time.

My father had to decide, and he did. "Go ahead and operate," he said. "I couldn't live with the guilt of not saving her life when I could have." So my mother underwent this low-risk procedure. And died on the operating table.

My father lived about another five years after my mother's death and he took care of himself just fine. Once I asked him about his decision. He said, "It was the best thing. I tried to save her life, so I didn't have to live with the guilt of not trying. And she never had to live in an institution. So I kept my good conscience and she kept her dignity."

## Honoring a Person's Wishes

If my father had pressed me to give him a direct answer, what would I have said?

While I believe in the sanctity of life, and believe that life is good and to be lived to its fullest, I don't think that life should always be prolonged. Life isn't always better than death. If my mother had understood her own condition, if she knew that she would have been like a child and reduced to complete dependency, if she were capable of knowing that she was putting a burden on my father emotionally and financially, if she knew that she would be in a nursing home perhaps for years, I think she would have chosen to end her life as gracefully as possible.

"Dad," I would have said, "Mom had a good life. It was a long one. Soon she won't be the same person she has always been. You know what she said about things like this. Some of your friends have Alzheimer's. She said she never wanted to be institutionalized or to have other people take care of her as though she were a baby. I think she would want to die now rather than burdening you with caring for her, a woman she never was and didn't want to become. If she could answer for herself right now, I think she would ask you to take her home and let nature take its course. You won't be killing her by doing this. You yourself have said that doctors shouldn't try to keep a person alive if it means that she will be more like a vegetable than a human being. Please, Dad, don't let them operate, for Mom's sake and yours."

# 12

✦

# Do I Reveal a Secret If I Think It Helps?

Randall, eighteen, suspects that his sister Lisa, sixteen, is adopted. He asks his parents if it is true. Reluctantly, they tell him that she was adopted. They had decided not to tell Lisa because they thought that it was best for her not to know. They want her to feel no different than any other child. They ask Randall to keep the secret. Randall disagrees with them about continuing to keep the information from Lisa and tries unsuccessfully to persuade them to change their minds. He decides to tell Lisa the secret about herself.

Some questions to ask yourself:

1. How do you decide what information to share with others?
2. If you know something about someone that they don't know about themselves, should you tell them?
3. If you believe that the secret you have been sworn to keep is now harmful, must you continue to keep quiet?
4. Under what conditions should a secret be revealed?
5. Is Randall doing the moral thing?

# The Problem:
# The Need for Knowledge

Nearly everyone has a secret. Some are fun, such as planning a surprise party. Some are trivial, such as liking trashy movies. Some are embarrassing, such as things done in private. Some, though, may be significant, such as having been previously married.

Small and trivial secrets don't amount to much. But big secrets often have a big impact even as they remain secret.

What do you do when you know something about someone that she may not even know herself? This is often a burden and a strain on a relationship. But is it ethical to reveal it?

# Family Secrets:
# Fear and Shame

A graphic and macabre example of a long-kept family secret became news during the testimony of Sabrina Yaw at a trial in New York City in 2000. For twenty-one years she had lived with a secret that began when she was nine. She said that she remembered watching her mother and older brother beat her baby sister to death, then place the body in a wooden trunk that was put in a bedroom closet. Sabrina kept her sister's murder a secret because she feared for her own life. She revealed what she knew only when a brother approached her with suspicions that he once had a twin sister who had disappeared years before, when he was too young to remember. Only then did Sabrina tell Andre what she knew. Even then she swore him to secrecy. Andre was horrified and immediately went to the police, who found the mummified body in the family's apartment.

Family secrets are rarely as dramatic as this one, but something like it must have given rise to the expression "having a skeleton in the closet." Where there are secrets, there are alliances; where there are secrets, there are insiders and outsiders; where there are secrets, there are suspicions; where there are secrets, there are deceptions, half-truths, cover-ups, and lies. All this has an impact on how a family functions.

Family secrets are commonplace. They may be minor, such as hiding having had cosmetic surgery, or they may be major, such as not telling a spouse about having other children. Secrets often involve matters that are considered shameful or too hurtful to reveal. Mental illness, drug addiction, and physical or sexual abuse frequently go unspoken about. While adoption is more open than it has ever been, it remains a secret for some.

# Adoption:
# Why There Are Secrets

I have a special interest in secrets about adoption because my wife and I have an adopted daughter who is now grown with a family of her own. In 1966, attitudes regarding adoption were just beginning to change. Most adoptees were still shielded from a significant fact of their own lives, but our social worker's advice to us was that we should talk about our daughter's adoption early on. It shouldn't be treated as though it were something shameful that should only be revealed with time. Despite this openness, there was still a secret surrounding the adoption. We were given very little information about Kori's birth parents. The records were sealed. This wasn't for our daughter's sake, but for the sake of the biological parents, to protect their privacy. For what wasn't shameful to us might have been shameful to them.

# Keeping Secrets:
# Weighing Benefits and Harms

The morality of holding secrets regarding adoption comes down to this: who benefits and who gets hurt? If an adopted child wants to know the identity of her biological parents and is granted such information, she might contact them, thereby reminding them of what they may not like to think about. Who knows but they may never have consented to the adoption if they had known that someday their identity would be revealed. So promises were made to them, for better or for worse, and those promises are still honored today. Of course, the adopted child never consented to this agreement, but infants never consent to arrangements adults enter into.

Since we don't know very much about Lisa's family in the story, let's assume that they kept her adoption secret because they thought it was in her best interest, not because they were ashamed of what some might perceive as their failure to have "their own child." The secret, then, isn't for their sake but for the sake of the child.

Paternalistic secrets in families are fairly commonplace. A person who has been diagnosed with AIDS may choose to keep this knowledge from the rest of the family, to spare them the anguish of knowing the truth that someone they love has a grave illness that carries a social stigma. Or a family may know that one of their members has a terminal cancer, and with the complicity of the doctor, keep this information from the patient himself.

I knew a woman who was in a home hospice but the family never told her that it was anything more than temporary nursing. Until two days before she died she talked to me about getting back on her feet. Her family, I suppose, wanted to keep her spirits up, so she never talked to me about her impending death. This, I believe, deprived her of what could have been a rich experience.

But this was her daughter's choice—to not tell her mother the truth—and it wasn't for me to upend the deception.

## Knowledge: Power and Trust

I asked a psychotherapist who specializes in individuals and families what she thought about Lisa's not being told about her adoption. Sherry Hartwell, who practices in San Diego, says, "Lisa's parents intended no harm. They wanted to protect Lisa and the integrity of the family as a whole. Inadvertently, the parents may have made the situation worse because they could not see Lisa's potential for handling incrementally the adoption facts as she was growing up."

Hartwell's point is a basic one: Knowledge is power, and when we deprive someone of significant knowledge, we have power over them that may do them harm. "Unfortunately," Hartwell continues, "Randall, Lisa, and Lisa's parents did not have the benefit of the current attitudes and approaches to the process of adoption that society has come to accept. However, these new attitudes provide a particular background or context for this family's reconsideration of the secrecy of Lisa's adoption."

Randall, frustrated by his parents' refusal to tell his sister the truth about her biological roots, forces the issue by giving Lisa this information about herself. Randall seems to share the current thinking on adoption: tell the truth. He first goes to his parents. After all, they imposed the silence. But they won't listen to him. So he takes matters into his own hands.

"Randall in developing his own values has become adamant that the truth be told," Hartwell says. "But he does not yet know much about this truth, nor can he foresee how telling will impact the family. What the family now faces is both the fact that Lisa was adopted and the deception surrounding it."

Randall, in revealing the secret, creates a new set of conditions. "The fundamental experience of trust or lack of trust is part of the crisis in this family. Randall's decision will affect the family as a whole and each individual in ways that cannot be foreseen. It is likely that the fundamental issue of trust will be repeatedly brought into question as the family members process this emotional and psychological crisis. Randall's action offers the possibility of a family coming to terms with a secret and developing new capacities—psychologically, emotionally, and morally." Hartwell continues, "Randall's insistence on telling Lisa the truth will most likely lead to different understandings of Lisa's and Randall's upbringing."

## A Moral Dilemma:
## Respect versus Responsibility

Randall's moral dilemma is that of being caught between respecting his parents' wishes and his responsibility to his sister, between being trustworthy and being truthful. Assuming that Randall cares about Lisa, his telling her is an expression of his love for her, not a sign of disrespect for his parents. If he thinks that she is disadvantaged because of her ignorance and that she will be better off with the knowledge of her adoption, then it is right that he tell her despite his parents' wishes.

There is no way of predicting what will happen once Randall tells. "The outcome will depend on how well each family member manages the emotional upheavals each will feel," Hartwell notes. "The dangers are great. Family members in the face of a crisis can cut off from one another emotionally for some period of time."

It seems to me that two things are plausible: the parents will be relieved of the burden of deception and they will be furious with Randall. It's also possible that Lisa will feel relieved once she gets over the shock. (It is hard to believe that she has had no hunch she was adopted.) However, there is also the risk that the parents will feel that they can't any longer trust their son. Furthermore, there is the possibility of a more extreme reaction from Lisa. She may be so overwhelmed by the news that she will be angry and sever her relationship with the entire family.

There are risks either way. Yet it is hard to imagine that Lisa would be in the dark her entire life. Sooner or later she is bound to find out about her adoption. For example, what would her parents tell her when a doctor asks about her family history so she can assess the possible risks of inheritable diseases? Hartwell makes this point a little more generally: "Lisa has been deprived of choice(s) related to gaining knowledge of her biological parents. This keeps her from acting authentically as an agent on her own behalf." People have a right to information about themselves. Without such information they are deprived of the ability to lead their own lives as they see most fit. Respect is a central moral value, and keeping back this information from Lisa is to distrust her ability to conduct her own life.

# Acting:
## Taking a Guess about the Future

There is also a practical point here. Someone, sometime will let the secret slip. If three people are in on a secret, chances are that there are really more than three. It is better that Lisa find out the truth about herself from someone who cares rather than stumbling across it without the benefit of having a loved one there to cushion the shock, to offer support, to put it into context.

Generally speaking, family secrets are harmful to good human relations. I believe this strongly when it comes to adoption. It is best for everyone when the adoption is spoken about openly and is accepted as merely another fact in the family history.

Randall took a chance in talking to Lisa. He should be commended for it—provided he did it generously and with sensitivity. If he was motivated not by love for his sister but by something else, such as jealousy and the desire to place her further on the outside, then his actions would be judged differently. But I am assuming that Randall does care about his sister and that he wants the best for her, and he tells her for her own sake, not his own. I hope his parents can accept his act of defiance as an expression of his love for his sister. In my experience, when a family secret is exposed in a caring manner, the family is stronger for it. People grow closer together when they can forgive one another. The newfound honesty in the family may lay a better foundation than the one they now have for a healthy, workable emotional intimacy, one that has been cleared of the tangle of deceit and half-truths.

# 13

~⚬~

# Is It Moral for Me to Help Someone Commit Suicide?

Janet is suffering from Lou Gehrig's disease, a fatal illness that affects the body but not the mind. The disease advances through progressive paralysis. Janet, who still can speak, is only able to move her head from side to side. She knows that within a few weeks she will no longer be able to breathe, and will therefore die.

Janet asks her husband, Mario, to give her all the pills at her bedside so that she may die now. He agrees with her wish but he doesn't have the nerve to give them to her.

Janet's clergyman visits. She asks him to help hasten her death. He declines to do so. Janet dies two weeks later, having succumbed to her illness after much mental anguish.

Some questions to ask yourself:

1. Is killing always wrong?
2. Is life worth living under all circumstances?
3. Should a person have the right to decide for herself whether to live or die?
4. Is it ever right to help someone die?

5. Is it ever right to break the law to help someone else?
6. Is the clergyman doing the right thing?

## The Problem: Alleviating Suffering versus a Culture of Death

Suicide is a form of murder—the taking of one's own life. To involve another person in a suicide is to make someone an accomplice to a crime. That's the law, more or less. But nearly everyone considers suicide less a legal offense than a moral matter. We don't jail failed suicides as felons.

The same logic that assumes suicide to be unlawful applies from an ethical point of view. Certainly if suicide is wrong, then involving another person must also be morally wrong. However, not everyone thinks that suicide is morally wrong. Even so, granting that it isn't a moral wrong, the question is still open of whether it is immoral to involve another person in the suicide.

Holland has adopted the most liberal policy in this regard, which some see as establishing a culture of death. Others consider it a humane way to resolve a dreadful situation. Hastening death is preferable to prolonged misery.

I had to confront this problem not as an abstract concern in a classroom or a secondhand one by developing hospital policy, but as a request made of me by someone who wanted to die. Janet and Mario (pseudonyms) were members of my congregation for many years. During the course of a pastoral visit, she asked me to give her enough medication so she could kill herself.

"I want to die now," she said to me plaintively. "I would take the pills myself, but I can't, and Mario won't give them to me." She said that it was like waiting to be executed, and that the anticipation of her inevitable death within about a week was torture. This was the most heart-wrenching request I had ever received.

# Helping Someone Die

My friend and colleague Joe Chuman faced a similar situation in his own religious community. A member of his congregation also had amyotrophic lateral sclerosis, more commonly known as Lou Gehrig's disease. "If nature were malicious, it could not devise a more sadistic path leading to life's end," he says. The woman he visited explained the disease more graphically to him than Janet did to me: "The paralysis starts at the feet and gradually ascends to the torso and upper body. Death is inevitable. It comes either through starvation, as the voluntary ability to swallow is destroyed, or through suffocation, as the lungs relentlessly fill up with fluid."

One day, when her illness was far along, this woman confronted Chuman with the same request that Janet had made of me. "As I sat by her bedside one afternoon, Margaret [a pseudonym] told me how she feared most an invasion of her bodily integrity. She wanted no part of ventilators or feeding tubes. With her options drastically diminished, she turned to me, in whom she had developed a strong trust, and without a ripple of hesitation, asked whether I would help her administer an overdose of medication."

Chuman and I had to decide two things: Did we approve of suicide, and if we did, were we willing to assist in a suicide?

There is no question about the second question if you disapprove of the first. So I'm going to begin by looking at the morality of suicide.

# Some Suicides Are Called Martyrs

There is a long tradition against suicide in the Western world. Until the last century, those who committed suicide were buried not with ordinary folk but alongside those convicted of witchcraft and murder. Suicide was understood as murder against oneself. Aristotle opposed suicide; Kant condemned it. The Catholic Church has long condemned it, with Augustine referring to the sixth of the Ten Commandments and Aquinas viewing it as contrary to the natural law whereby every person should love himself. At the same time, there has been another tradition that accepts suicide under certain circumstances, as most visitors to Israel know. There, at the top of a hill, stands Masada, the site of an entire community of martyrs who chose to die at their own hands rather than surrender to the Roman army. Contrary to Jewish tradition, they are not condemned but are honored as heroes. The more common use of ritual suicide in Japan, even into this century, is also founded on the sense of honor. It is better to die an honorable death at one's own hand than to live a life in dishonor and shame.

Suicide, then, like killing, may be condemned in general but still admit exceptions. What are those exceptions?

The most fundamental reason murder is morally reprehensible is that it violates the rule of respect for people. But there is more to respect than preventing harm. It also means that a person has a right to decide what she wants to make of her own life. It is precisely because we respect people that we extend the rights to free speech, religion, movement, and assembly. The state can interfere with matters of conscience only under extreme circumstances, when the integrity of society itself is at stake. That is what is meant by respect for persons—the right to autonomy and self-determination.

## Moral Choices Require Choosing Wisely

This isn't to say that everything we choose to do with our freedom is moral, though. Clearly it isn't. Some things may be morally neutral, having little or no moral weight, such as whether to picnic at the beach or in a park. What this means is that there are two levels of morality at work at the same time: the social level, which grants the right to self-determination; and the personal level, which is concerned with what we choose to do with the freedom we have. A moral society is one that rests upon the protection of such civil liberties; a moral person is one who acts responsibly toward others. Some people abuse the freedoms they have—they do crackpot or stupid things. But in a moral society they have the right to be a crackpot and act stupidly.

At the same time, there are some things that we aren't free to choose. We can't choose to be slaves, for example. Slavery is wrong even if it is entered into voluntarily. Slavery violates the very essence of what it means to be human. So is suicide in the same category as slavery, something we aren't free to choose because to choose it would be to contradict our own freedom?

One argument against suicide makes exactly that point. Society doesn't allow irrational people to do whatever they want, even when not harming others, since they don't always understand what is in their own best interest. By definition, anyone who chooses suicide must be irrational because the act itself ends all possibilities of self-determination. Therefore a person ought be prevented from carrying out her wishes, because killing oneself leads to excluding all future choices.

While suicide is considered homicide in many places, typically it isn't treated as such by the state. One reason is that we don't make criminals of the insane. Also, nothing would be gained by prosecuting the offender. Suicidal people aren't criminally motivated, in the sense that their actions aren't meant to take something away from someone else. They are far more likely to be depressed, which is clouding their ability to think clearly. According to Herbert Hendin, the medical director of the American Foundation for Suicide Prevention, "nearly 95 percent of all people who kill themselves have a psychiatric illness diagnosable in the months before suicide. The majority suffer from depression, which can be treated." And when the depression lifts and he is "more himself," suicide recedes as an option. Hendin's point is that most suicides are attempted by people who "aren't in their right minds."

## A Rational Suicide

But what about the remaining percent who, according to Hendin, don't have a psychiatric illness but still want to kill themselves? Something else entirely may be going on. In fact, not all decisions to end one's life are considered irrational. We even applaud some who choose their own deaths. The highest medals awarded by the military are for those who sacrifice themselves for the sake of others—the soldier who smothers a grenade with his body; the Marine who holds a position so others can retreat safely, the pilot who doesn't parachute to safety and instead guides his plane away from a town. This type of suicide is actually commended. To die for the sake of another—self-sacrifice—is the highest form of love, according to Christian ethics.

So killing oneself isn't always immoral. The soldier is esteemed because he intended to save a life, not because he wanted to die. His death was a secondary result of the primary purpose.

The self-killing that morally bothers us is the kind in which a rational person chooses to end her own life not for the sake of others or a cause that we endorse but because she wants to end her own suffering.

Another clergyman friend of mine, Geoffrey, once told me about the funeral of a childhood friend of his. The man committed suicide in the face of a fatal illness. As a Christian minister, Geoffrey said that his religion taught him that suicide is immoral. However, he knew his friend well and he knew that he was not a sinful person.

Far from it. So at the service at which he officiated, he couldn't condemn his friend. This was a good person who had died. The man had suffered from an incurable illness and had chosen to taken his own life. As far as Geoffrey was concerned, no sin was involved.

Discussion and anxiety about this type of suicide occur in the context of advances in medicine. The sad fact is that we know how to prolong life but we cannot always extend dignity. As a result, we have people living longer, many of whom cannot care for themselves, are drained of all pleasure, suffer mental anguish, and find life without meaning.

## The Right to Refuse Treatment

Hospitals have come close to acknowledging the right of patients to kill themselves. Patients are free to reject treatment, even when medical opinion is that without the procedure the person will surely die. The right to refuse treatment is written into the patient's bill of rights and has been extended to allow a patient's surrogate, for example, to order tubes to be disconnected even when death will inevitably follow. In other words, society now acknowledges that choosing to die isn't always irrational or immoral.

I am a member of the ethics committee at Winthrop University Hospital on Long Island. Every month we listen to reports about a patient refusing the only treatment that will keep him alive or a wife's discontinuing life support for her husband. Some physicians acknowledge off the record that when they send home a terminally ill patient with a month's supply of medication, they know that the medication is often used as a means to commit suicide.

When my mother-in-law, Rose, was terminally ill, one day she and my wife and the physician discussed removing the feeding tubes and giving her morphine to control the pain. It was clear to all of us that as the morphine dosage was increased to control her pain, her breathing would be compromised. Mom never explicitly said that she wanted to die, but it was clear that she understood the consequences of her decision. We sat at her bedside that evening and said good-bye to one another before she fell into a coma. Rose died ten hours later. My mother-in-law had chosen her own death, her own way, at her own time.

What Mom did was no more a suicide than the laudable act of a soldier, since the intent of giving her morphine was to control her pain, not to kill her, although death was certain. This is a very fine distinction, but one worth keeping in mind. It reminds us that we don't always measure the ethical rightness of something in terms of consequences. Motives also count. But when Rose decided to substitute morphine for medication, she didn't merely choose to lessen her pain, but also decided to die.

## Compassion and Respect

What, then, are the ethics of suicide? Given the considerations mentioned previously, I believe that it would be unethical to prevent adults from choosing their own deaths, provided that all steps have been taken to ensure that the suicide is not the result of a treatable depression. Choosing to die can be a legitimate choice, one that society doesn't condemn but accepts as a tragic aspect of life.

*Helping* someone to die, however, raises additional moral questions. If Janet and Margaret had been in a hospital receiving treatment to sustain their lives, they could have gotten what they wanted. Sometimes giving a patient enough morphine to control her pain can have the secondary result of causing her death. Ironically, Janet was at home, but she had less control over her own fate. I since have listened to doctors discuss such cases, and it may well be that Janet's doctors recognized that she might choose to end her own life and left enough pills at her beside to kill her. The problem was that because of her paralysis, she needed someone to put them in her mouth.

If withholding treatment can be seen as a compassionate act, so, too, can assisting someone to commit suicide. Both Chuman and I feel this keenly. As ministers, we are called upon to comfort those in great distress. But would it be right for us to break the law to do so? Chuman says, "The United States has had a long tradition of dissent, which is based on a profound respect for individual conscience. In rare instances of compelling moral import, after we have informed ourselves of the issues fully, and reflect on them as broadly and deeply as we can, we are obligated to break the law in order to be faithful to higher moral values."

## Breaking the Law

"The compelling nature of Margaret's awful disease," Chuman says, "its certain end in her death, and the intensely personal nature of her decision, which I do believe ought to be beyond the absolute reach of the state, made a prevailing claim on me. I was also her clergyman, whom she had come to rely on, which evokes a special relationship with particular duties. My relationship with Margaret provided such an instance in which breaking the law is justified."

While I agree with Chuman about breaking the law, I am not convinced that it was justified here. Part of my reason is what actually happened to Margaret. Chuman says, "My response to Margaret's request to aid her in dying was to tell her emphatically that I would help her in any way that I could. I was willing to grant her wish to assist in her suicide. Margaret, however, died two months later in bed, at home. Despite her earlier refusal, she had agreed to accept a feeding tube inserted in her abdomen, and there was a small respirator on her night table by the bed. As her condition overtook her, her digestive system began to fail and her breathing grew more labored. Margaret's doctor, a compassionate man who supported physician-assisted suicide as a last resort, was, nevertheless, able to persuade her that a gastrointestinal tube fell short of an extraordinary measure. And the small respirator was not permanent. It was there for use only when she felt she needed it."

## Controlling Pain and Providing Comfort

Margaret's choice wasn't unusual. Studies conducted in hospice settings have found that when patients are listened to and feel valued, when their pain is controlled, when significant people in their lives are involved, they feel that life is meaningful and their level of hope increases. It isn't the false hope that they will get better or leave the hospice. Rather it is a more generalized sense of well-being. Life is good and precious, despite the realities of impending death. As Dr. Hendin explains, "Patients do not know what to expect and cannot foresee how their condition will unfold as they decline toward death. Facing this uncertainty, they fill the vacuum with their fantasies and fears. When these fears are dealt with by a caring, knowledgeable physician, the request for an expedited death usually disappears."

I don't know about Margaret's family life, nor can I understand the depth of her relationship with Chuman. But Janet had a husband and two grown daughters. I refused Janet's request because I thought that I didn't have the moral standing to help her end her life. That belonged to her family, under the supervision of a doctor. The only person who could have acted as a surrogate was her husband. The minister's role—the one I adopted—was to help her to understand and accept her death. The comfort that was mine to bring was something other than the administration of poison. I could help the husband understand her wishes, but I had no moral standing to do what he could not bring himself to do.

Janet lived another week. Her suffering that week, which I had the power to alleviate but did not, has bothered me ever since.

Two thousand years ago Seneca wrote, "If I can choose between a death of torture and one that is simple and easy, why should I not select the latter? As I choose the ship in which I sail and the house which I inhabit, so will I choose the death by which I leave life."

Janet had the right to choose the ship upon which she would sail to a port unknown. But no one had the duty or right to help her, except her husband. Only he had the moral authority to put her on that ship.

When Janet asked me to help her, I turned to her husband. When he refused, there was no more that I could or should do.

## 14

❧

# Does My Child Have the Right to Privacy?

Fifteen-year-old Anthony recently has been moody and sullen. His parents are worried, but Anthony will not talk to them about what is bothering him. His grades have gone down and his parents are worried that he may be suicidal. One day he is on the telephone with the door closed. It sounds to his parents as if he is confiding to a friend, but they can't make out what he is saying. They decide to eavesdrop by listening in on an extension.

Some questions to ask yourself:

1. What are the relevant facts for Anthony's parents to consider?
2. Should parents have the right to set the rules about what happens in their home?
3. Does the right to privacy apply to children?
4. How far should parents go in protecting the well-being of their teenage child?
5. Would you make a different judgment if Anthony were older?
6. What if he were younger?

7. Do parents have the right to know everything about their child?

8. Do you think that Anthony's parents are making the right moral choice?

# The Problem:
## Protecting Privacy versus Acting on Partial Knowledge

If you are a parent, you worry about your child. It comes with the territory. And your anxiety increases as your child reaches adolescence. It's a tough time for both of you. Just as your daughter tries to figure out who she is, what she believes, and what kind of person she wants to become, she is also extremely sensitive and vulnerable. Peer pressure is enormous, and it is natural for her to physically and psychologically distance herself from you. Her emotions are sometimes at a fever pitch and sometimes they plummet into the depths of loneliness and despair.

All this gives you good reason to worry. In all likelihood, though, despite the tears and traumas, she will be all right. Most teenagers survive adolescence fine. Unfortunately, increasing numbers of teenagers are unable to cope with these stresses. For them suicide seems to be a way out of the depression in which they find themselves. The Centers for Disease Control and Prevention, in a 2000 study, reported that 8 percent of all American students from elementary through high school attempted suicide within the year and another 20 percent thought about it. This means that more than one-quarter of all students have flirted with the idea of ending their own lives. Suicide is the third leading cause of death in people between fifteen and twenty-four, surpassing all illnesses. On Long Island, where I live, the Long Island Crisis Center receives more than four thousand calls a year from teenagers contemplating suicide. So Anthony's parents' worry isn't such the exaggerated concern of overinvolved parents.

# Privacy:
# Do Children Have Such a Right?

Are Anthony's parents justified in picking up the telephone to listen in on a conversation that they think will give them a better understanding of their son's true state of mind? I asked Barbara Ehrenreich, a noted social critic who spends a lot of time thinking about relationships in the modern world.

Ehrenreich and I disagree on a number of points. Her first point is philosophical, as she makes a moral claim.

"Eavesdropping is a mistake," she said. "First, because it is a violation of Anthony's privacy—and teenagers, even sullen ones, do have a right to privacy."

But do teenagers who live in their parents' house have a right to privacy? I wonder. Here I partially agree with Ehrenreich. It's fair to say that Anthony and his parents think that he does. He has a telephone in his own bedroom, for example. People have telephones in their rooms not merely for convenience but also so that they can talk privately. Privacy in the last several centuries has become an important value, protecting against the intrusiveness of others and thereby offering a person possibilities of leading the life he wants, not the one others want for him.

Privacy, in other words, is one way of respecting the human personality. Very young children aren't granted privacy. They need to have their diapers changed and to be looked in on when the parent wants. But Anthony isn't an infant any longer, and as good parents will acknowledge, the zone of privacy is increased. His growing autonomy as an individual is fostered by his ability, for example, to reveal or conceal his emotional life from his parents' intrusion. To become a unique, mature person, he needs to establish new boundaries in relation to his parents.

## Privacy: Is It Absolute?

Is Anthony's right to privacy absolute? Privacy has been honored in the family because his parents have accepted it as desirable. To some extent it fosters a sense of control over one's own life. However, in cases of emergency, strictly adhering to rules or keeping promises may result in hideous consequences. If privacy impedes the family's desired ultimate goals (and keeping Anthony alive is certainly one of them), then it is subject to reconsideration. Although Anthony is a near-adult, he does not—and perhaps never will—have an equal vote in ultimate decisions affecting the family.

So while I think Anthony has a right to privacy, I don't think it is an absolute or unqualified right.

His parents believe that he will kill himself unless they know what he is thinking and feeling. If their hunch about him is right and if Anthony succeeds, the results will be dire and irrevocable. Therefore, it is morally legitimate for the parents to overturn a family rule without Anthony's consent, especially since Anthony won't talk to them about the perceived problem.

I agree with philosopher Jeffrey Blustein's statement regarding the role of parents. "In assessing any social practice of child rearing," he writes, "you have to consult three separate, legitimate, and interrelated types of interests: those of the child, those of the child-rearers, and those of society. The legitimate interests of the child include an interest in physical care, in education and socialization, and in the warmth, consistency, and continuity of the relationship he has with the person who takes care of him."

So while Anthony has correctly come to expect that his privacy will not be violated in his home by his parents and therefore can talk on the telephone without them eavesdropping, he has also come to expect that they will take care of him.

# Eavesdropping:
## A Practical Consideration and a Guess

Ehrenreich's second objection looks at Anthony's parents' motives. Here she makes a psychological argument. She says that "the assumption seems to be that *knowing* what the problem is—at least as Anthony defines it to a friend—is essential to helping *solve* the problem. I suspect his parents may be a tiny bit jealous that he didn't pick them to talk to. They are so desperate to be included and involved that they are willing to trespass on the private space in which Anthony maintains his friendship. By eavesdropping, they will only be evading the real challenge—which is to rebuild their own lines of communication with their son."

Ehrenreich's third objection is practical. She doesn't think that parents can find out useful information by snooping. The real danger, as she sees it, is that the eavesdropping may make things worse. Anthony will view his parents as untrustworthy. "He may withdraw further," she says, "possibly making it harder for any adult—a therapist or member of the clergy, for example—to reach him. Almost certainly, his parents 'spying' will now count among his many grievances against the world. This is the challenge: to reconnect with Anthony and do it soon."

Ehrenreich and I agree that Anthony's well-being is primary. She believes connections between parents and children are essential, as I do. However, we part company over the distance parents must keep between themselves and their offspring.

# The Desire to Protect: How Far Does a Parent Go to Get Information?

Anthony's parents listen in on the extension because they believe they need vital information about their son for his own sake that he refuses to disclose to them. Without that information, they think they cannot help him. Without their help, they fear he may commit suicide.

They don't know why Anthony has become uncommunicative; they don't know why his grades have fallen. They are afraid for his life. They believe, rightly, that as his parents they have an obligation to keep him alive.

Although there are good reasons to limit the power of the state to interfere with the liberty of an individual, parent-child relationships are different. Society requires parents to exercise power over their children even though it may be contrary to the child's wishes. We have an obligation to educate our children even if they want to sleep late and watch TV all day. In fact, a parent who does not exercise proper control is liable both for the harm done *by* and *to* the child as a result of inadequate supervision. Society holds parents responsible for their child's welfare and therefore holds them accountable for both abuse and neglect. Parents are culpable for what harm they may cause (abuse) and also for what harm they fail to prevent (neglect).

# Affection and Care
## versus Rules and Rights

Ehrenreich fears that spying could drive more of a wedge between Anthony and his parents than may already be there. It may be that

Anthony will be angry with his parents for meddling. But equally plausible is that he will find a sense of relief and reassurance, if in fact he is suicidal. And even if he isn't, he may appreciate (perhaps later as an adult and parent himself) his parents' concern, even if it turns out to be misguided in this particular case.

The bonds of love and care are primary values in family matters; privacy is a secondary value, one we accept because it helps achieve our primary ones. I'm not suggesting that parents do whatever they want. But if Anthony's parents have betrayed the principle of privacy, they have done it to preserve another principle: preventing grave harm to their child.

The case forces me to make certain assumptions that, if they turn out to be wrong, would alter my assessment. First, I assume that Anthony's parents have made serious attempts to talk to Anthony about their concern. Second, I assume that they do not regularly invade his privacy and that now they do so reluctantly, in full knowledge that it violates another standard. Third, I assume that they have consulted experts about teenage suicide so that they can be sure that they are not reacting merely to their anxieties about his growing up. Fourth, I assume that Anthony's behavior isn't typical for him and is decidedly different from normal teenage behavior. And fifth, I assume that their actions are motivated by a love for their son and that the family members in all other ways respect one another.

Ideally, affection and care, not rules and rights, bind families. Rules and rights arise in more impersonal social institutions where people are bound together for reasons other than simply caring about one another. People in these institutions often need formal protections against the self-interested actions of others they come into contact with.

So while I think the right to privacy is an important value, in families care is the more important value. Interfering with Anthony's privacy was justified, in my opinion, because parents shouldn't allow children to kill themselves.

When it comes to young people in particular, most of us accept the wisdom of the psychotherapist Herbert Hendin, who says, "An attempted suicide is not an effort to die but rather is a communication to others in an effort to improve one's life."

# 15

❧

# Should I Compete against Friends?

Brad and Kevin are good friends. They both enjoy running. However, there is only one opening on the school track team. Brad, the far superior of the two runners, decides not to try out because he knows that if he does, Kevin won't make the team, and he knows how important it is to Kevin to make the team.

Some questions to ask yourself:

1. Should friends compete with one another?
2. In your scale of values, how important is friendship?
3. Is friendship a more important value than success?
4. How do you define success?
5. Is Brad making the right moral choice?

## The Problem:
## Competition versus Friendship

Friendship requires certain qualities—generosity, forgiveness, sincerity, and loyalty among them. These traits are necessary for sustained, close relationships. But society often expects different values from us. In order to succeed, we need a minimum level of ambition and the willingness to compete. But what happens when these two sets of values are present in the same place at the same time?

When I heard this story about Kevin and Brad, I thought about the two Roman philosophers and friends, Damon and Pythias. Pythias was sentenced to die because of his plot against the life of King Dionysius I of Syracuse. However, he wanted to return home to arrange family matters before his execution, so his friend Damon persuaded the king to hold him prisoner in his friend's stead. "If Pythias doesn't come back, take my life instead," he told the king. The day of the execution arrived and Damon prepared himself for death when, at the last moment, Pythias returned. Dionysius I was so moved by the friends' willingness to die for each other that he pardoned Pythias and begged to become part of their philosophical circle.

Perhaps Kevin's coach will take his cue from Dionysius I and find a place for both friends on the team. But you know that won't happen. After all, Damon and Pythias lived 2,400 years ago. Times have changed. Besides, no one knows if the story is even true. The real world, I'm told, doesn't work that way at all. Friends don't offer their lives for one another; a person doesn't give up his place on a team because his friend wants it more than he does. Each person should do the best that he can and let the friendship chips fall where they will. The right thing to do is to try our best. It is wrong to give up our place, our reward, to someone who isn't as good as we are. Being good means doing our best. It has nothing to do with being a good person.

# Male and Female Values

Yet we all recognize that friendship is an important value. Our lives would be poorer without a good friend. And most of us would really value a friend who was willing to give us a gift and would be honored if the gift was heartfelt. So what happens when the value of friendship clashes with the values of success and competition? What happens to someone like Brad, who wants to be a good friend, a good person in the second sense of the word— that is, he is loyal to his friend. Brad is genuinely a "nice" guy in the fullest sense of that word. Leo Durocher gave his answer when he said, "Good guys finish last." *New York Times* sports columnist Harvey Araton once wrote, "Monuments and trophy cases are built faster for jocks who score than for champions of virtue."

Durocher may not reflect everyone's attitude toward winning. Women seem to have a different approach, says Diana Nyad, a former world champion swimmer and now radio commentator on National Public Radio. "Most male coaches of male youth teams need the win too badly to play the inferior kids when the big game is on the line," Nyad says. "On the other hand, most female coaches of female youth teams deem it more important for every girl on the team to play some part." Nyad continues, "For women, sports have meant freedom—freedom from the constricting Victorian garb, freedom from the shackles of perpetual pregnancy, freedom to get an education. For men, sports have meant a proving grounds for comparative worth within the society."

When Nyad looks at the situation presented here, she says, "Brad has engaged in a traditionally female approach and behavior. If he had taken the traditional male approach, he would have considered the record of his school first. The track team—and the good name of his school—would have received more honors within the community, a better chance for quality recruitment, and more respect within the school itself, had Brad participated instead of Kevin."

It is precisely for these reasons that I admire Brad so much. For him friendship is more important than sports. That he chooses friendship over competition and success is what I find so appealing about his decision.

## Quality, Efficiency, and Human Relations

So Leo Durocher's sentiment may be popular only among males. It also may be factually incorrect. Not only may there be no conflict between being nice and being successful, but being successful may have something to do with being nice. Let's take a look at business. Studies done of organizations indicate that generally three factors contribute to the success of any business, group, or association: quality, efficiency, and decent human relations. All three are needed in varying degrees, depending upon the nature of the group. It isn't merely that someone can do or make the best (he may also be obsessively meticulous and plodding) or can turn out the most (she may be sloppy). The third factor is the intangible human one, the chemistry between people, the ambience that makes people want to be there. People have to work well together, treat one another more or less decently, and feel an important part of the overall effort. This is why a good personnel officer who keeps employees relatively happy and satisfied often turns out to be a key to a company's long-term success.

A number of years ago, in the professional basketball draft, the country's most talented player was nearly the last taken. Despite his impressive statistics and demonstrated ability in college, he had a reputation for being difficult, egotistical, moody, and emotionally erratic. It wasn't that the pros thought he wouldn't produce for them but that his presence on the team would be so disruptive that he would be a liability, not an asset. His temper tantrums almost outweighed his considerable athletic prowess, as far as the NBA was concerned. It really had nothing to do with ethics, for the ultimate value is still winning. We see this when violent, racist players are kept because they contribute to the team's successes, despite their unethical antics.

## Giving Up One's Life for Another

The Damon and Pythias legend is enduring and compelling because the friends were willing to die for each other. Although nothing is more important than preserving life and none more valuable than one's own, sometimes life is most honored by giving it up for someone else. Voluntarily dying for another is exemplary. It does depend, however, upon particular circumstances.

I've wondered about such loyalty and have occasionally asked people what or who they are willing to die for. The only consistent answer is: "My children." But even this response is hedged, subject to contingencies.

"It depends upon how old my children are," is the qualifier. "Sure, I'd sacrifice my life for my children at two or ten. But if they are twenty-five or thirty, I'm not so sure."

This reflects a cultural disposition, which expects parental sacrifice for the lives of little ones, but contemporary society is far more lenient about expecting sacrificial acts for one's adult children. Indeed, we think that there is something peculiar about parents who deny themselves pleasures in order to support their thirty-year-old son or daughter.

Sacrifice for the sake of friendship is different from family affairs. We make our friends, we can quit whenever we want, and there is nothing legally binding about the relationship. Families impose enforceable duties, but not so friendships. All that is found in a friendship issues from the heart. Still, hearts have perverse reasons known only to the unconscious.

# Competition:
## Are Men and Women Different?

I often find that it is useful when thinking about ethical problems to substitute different groups of people in the given situation. So I ask myself, would I have the same reaction to this vignette if Brad were a Brenda? Females are supposed to be self-sacrificing, and many women accept this role so readily that they don't even think about what they are giving up. I have seen many couples in marital therapy who once accepted this stereotypical behavior, where the wife put aside her own desires and goals in order to accommodate her husband's, but who now face a crisis because the wife is no longer content playing that part and the husband is baffled about what he sees as unwarranted and unreasonable new demands.

I don't know all that went into Brad's decision not to compete with Kevin for the position. Maybe Brad makes sacrifices all the time, maybe his self-sacrificing is part of a pattern in his life that reveals low self-esteem. Perhaps, subtly, Kevin intimidated Brad. But it doesn't strike me this way. Instead, I see a young man who is sensitive to his friend's needs and accepts them as more important than the accolades he may receive as a varsity runner.

Brad has given Kevin a gift. But not everyone thinks it is desirable to give such gifts. Anna Seaton Huntington, a two-time Olympic rower, writes that "the Olympic motto is faster, higher, stronger—not nicer. If [one friend backs] off, then what value would the gold medal have held for [his friend] if it had been a gift? . . . It is those rules, sometimes merciless, that allow them to measure themselves, to earn their self-respect."

What Huntington overlooks is that in a zero-sum competition, where there is only one winner, the self-respect of one person is often gained at the sense of failure on the part of everyone else. There is one winner while everyone else is a loser. If Brad tried out for the team, I fail to see how this would enhance Kevin's self-esteem. On the other hand, by Brad making way for Kevin, Brad can take pleasure in the way that anyone does who makes another happy.

Nyad also disagrees with Huntington. "Many thinkers have suggested that you might just put a stop to war if women became our leaders," she says. "And many sports sociologists have expressed the hope that women will bring their own ethics and standards as they enter into the superstar world of sports, instead of mimicking the men. So far, the women of the new professional basketball league, the Women's National Basketball League, have been humble, grateful, and graciously thrilled to be appreciated for their efforts and their talents. If boys and men start making these kinds of decisions, they too will help bring a valuable women's set of ethics and decision-making to men's sports."

## Good Sportsmanship

Damon and Pythius may be mythical, but Esther Kim and Kay Poe are not. Kim and Poe were good friends who were scheduled to meet in the taekwondo Olympic trials to decide which one of the two athletes would be going to Sydney for the games, as the United States would send only one woman. The friends were slated to compete against each other. However, in the match just before the two were to face each other, Poe dislocated her kneecap.

"I asked her, 'Look, Kay, what are you going to do? Look at your knee, Kay. What are you going to do?'

"She looked at me and she looked to the other side and said, 'You're just going to fight. You're going to fight.' I turned her face to look at me and I said, 'Kay, how are you going to fight? You can't even stand up. How are you going to fight?' Then she just started crying and crying.

"I had no thought in my head, [conceding] was something that came completely out of my heart, and it made me cry because I knew right then that I was going to tell her, 'Kay, let me just bow out to you.' It was so hard because this was something that I did dream about all my life. This was something that I wanted more than anything in the world.

"I looked at her and I said, 'Kay, why don't I just bow out?' She was like, 'What?' I said, 'Kay, just don't argue with me. Just listen to me.' I told her, 'Kay, I want to bow out. You can't stand up. You can't fight. It's not fair. If you went into the ring, I have two legs, you have one leg. You can't even stand up. That's not fair to take it away from you that way.' I told her, 'I love you. I support you. Both of us have so much heart today. I was on fire, you were on fire, but I think you should go to the Olympics. I want you to take that spot.'"

Kim said her decision was made in a heartbeat. "For the first time in my life I felt like a champion."

The International Olympic Committee thought she was a champion, too. Its president, Juan Antonio Samaranch, personally invited her and her family to Sydney to watch the games. Committee members gave her a standing ovation at a reception, and the Citizenship Through Sports Alliance selected her to receive the Citizenship Through Sports Award. (Poe, incidentally, lost in the first round.)

# A Good Friend

How Brad carries off his decision is nearly as important as the act itself. If he expects something in return or in any way makes Kevin feel guilty, then his action is tainted. I don't know how he can successfully do this, although Esther Kim shows that it can be done with grace and even love. Perhaps Brad's relationship with Kevin is different than was the female martial artists'. If his motivation wasn't as pure, then perhaps he shouldn't have made the sacrifice. This I can't determine unless I know more about the friendship than I do. But assuming that it is possible, then I want to cheer for him, just as the International Olympic Committee stood and cheered for Esther Kim. After all, sports at their best should be about teaching sportsmanship. What better example is there of sportsmanship than a gift from the heart to someone you love?

How lucky Kevin is to have made such a friend, and what a fine person Kevin must be to have a friend willing to do such an unselfish thing for him.

# 16

# What Do I Owe
# an Elderly Parent?

Pamela and Richard have just retired. A doctor tells them that because of the onset of senility, Pamela's eighty-five-year-old mother cannot continue to live alone. Despite the necessity of forgoing many personal plans and recognizing the strain it will put upon them, Pamela and Richard decide that they cannot put Pamela's mother into a nursing home. Instead they move her into a spare bedroom in their house.

Some questions to ask yourself:

1. What do children owe their parents?
2. Are grown children responsible for their parents' well-being?
3. Are positive feelings a necessary basis for obligations?
4. In what way, if any, should money play a part in determining obligations?
5. What sacrifices are reasonable in order to meet your obligations?
6. How do you balance your needs and that of your spouse with that of another family member?
7. Are Pamela and Richard doing the right thing?

# The Problem:
# The Biological versus the Ethical

It's interesting that in the Ten Commandments we are instructed in how to treat our parents but not how to raise our children. Honor your mother and your father, we are told. Perhaps there is no corresponding commandment telling parents how to treat a child because the minimum requirements don't need to be spelled out. Everywhere and always parents must feed, shelter, and clothe their young children. For if parents didn't care for their children, there would be no future generations. Certainly, without adult protection, children couldn't survive, and without children, the human race would disappear.

But I wonder about the source of obligation for children to watch out for their parents. It's not obvious. We might even say that the opposite is required—that the old must make way for the young; the tree needs pruning, the field must be cleared for the next crop. So the Fifth Commandment—honor your mother and father—finds its validation not in a biological necessity but in something very different. In a sense, the purpose of the commandment is to reverse the natural order, replacing biology with ethics. It is a rule that raises society to a human level, as it establishes an obligation that replaces the brute realities of nature with morality. As long as our parents are alive, we should honor them. In practice this means that when they can no longer take care of themselves, we, as their children, must take care of them.

This attitude is a mark of human civilization. Unlike other animals, humans don't leave the infirm behind when they move. There is no biological advantage for children to honor their parents. It is purely an ethical notion, serving not the needs of the species but our personal, religious, and social sense of what it means to be human.

# Caring for the Elderly: Tradition

But how do we take care of the elderly? In 1975, when I was living in Kenya, a couple of my African friends came to our house to visit. We had known the two brothers, Nyangati and Ongesa, for a while, and they would sometimes stop by when they were in town doing chores. We sat around our dining table for a good half hour. We chatted about a variety of things. Kenyans usually take a while to get to what they really want to know, but this time was different. There was a sense that we were entering new territory. Finally, after much hesitation and with reluctance, one of them said, "We have heard that in America there is something you do. But we can't believe that it's true." What were they referring to? "Do you mind if we ask you?" Nyangati said, as though embarrassed, not for himself, but for us. Not at all, my wife and I said.

"We were told that when a person gets old, in America you send them away to die."

I was taken aback by their comment. Did they really see Americans like that, engaged in euthanasia of the elderly? I had never thought of Americans' treatment of the old that way before, but it was true, in a sense. I tried to explain that America was different than Kenya, that when children got married they moved away from their parents, sometimes across the continent. This was nearly unheard-of for them. When a son got married in Kenya, he would move into a new house with his wife on the same property where he had always lived. Mother, father, and brothers were all within shouting distance, until they died. How different things are in the United States. Here not only do grown children want to leave home, but many parents prefer it this way. As if to bear out the truth of this, both my parents and my wife's parents had moved to Florida, a thousand miles away from our New York home.

"But what happens when they get old and need to be taken care of?" Ongesa asked. We told them about adult homes and nursing homes. Sometime after this conversation, we were visiting with Ongesa when suddenly a young boy rushed into the house shouting something we couldn't make out. Ongesa leaped to his feet and ran to the vegetable patch. We followed. When we arrived, several people were already there, including his brother Nyangati. Their elderly mother stood in the field, terrified. While hoeing, she had seen a snake and had called for help. Several of her sons—all grown with their own families—heard her shouts and within moments had gone to her aid.

Now we understood why the brothers were incredulous when we told them about parents and children living apart. Their worst picture of Americans had been confirmed: we didn't honor our mothers and fathers. We didn't even live nearby. Who would take care of them when they were threatened? Who would care for them when they were sick?

## Caring for the Elderly: Today

A startling fact about the United States today is that for most of us, the last person who will literally touch us will be a stranger— a nurse, an aide, a doctor. It won't be a husband or wife, brother or sister, child or grandchild, but a stranger, someone who is there because he or she is being paid. It is the ultimate triumph of the market economy over human relations.

Things have changed in Kenya since my wife and I first lived there, just as they have in the United States. Both Nyangati and Ongesa have sons who live far from the family compound. The young men are in Nairobi, 250 miles away, a day's journey from their parents' place. Neither Nyangati nor Ongesa will have all their children present when they falter. It isn't hard to imagine that in the near future Kenyans, like Americans, will die without their families around them.

My parents moved to Florida so they could have a more comfortable life, away from winters and numbing cold. They could enjoy their final years in a style that once was reserved for the rich. And I understand why Kenyans are moving away from their homesteads and to the city: that's where the work is, that's where the comforts are found. For the first time, they will know electricity and running water. Far more than ever in human history, the "good life" is within the reach of the ordinary person in many places around the globe.

Nyangati and Ongesa must have thought that we Americans throw our old folks away, putting them out with the trash. They simply couldn't grasp what an adult home or a nursing home is. In reality, for some a nursing home is the best choice available. Frail people can get better care when all the proper equipment is right at hand. Sick individuals can be monitored and checked properly by people who are trained in elder care.

## Knowing the Context

I had to explain the realities of American life as I understood them to my African friends in order for them to appreciate the choices we face in the United States. Making moral judgments without knowing the context is dangerous. We can judge one thing as good or bad only as we understand how it relates to some situation in particular. So I asked David Harmon what he thought about the decision faced by Richard and Pamela in this vignette. Harmon, the director of the counseling center at St. John's University in Queens, New York, said, "You have to give Pamela and Richard some modicum of history to get a clearer picture of the dilemma that they might have to confront."

Harmon is quite right. All our judgments are based upon assumptions we hold about what we think the reality is. When we don't have all the facts, we tend to fill them in, as Nyangati and Ongesa did, with what we believe to be the case. Harmon imagines two different possibilities for Pamela and Richard, and then reaches two different possible conclusions.

In the first scenario Pamela's mother, a few days after the death of her own husband, sells the house in which she was living to Pamela and Richard for one dollar. They had previously lived in an apartment, which had been just big enough for their family. Pamela is her only child and she had always liked Richard. The idea of someone else, some strangers, living in the house that she and her husband had occupied for so many years was distressing. Pamela, after all, is used to the house, having grown up there. Her mother then moves into a small apartment near Pamela and Richard. The efficiency apartment is easier to take care of than the house in which she had formerly lived.

Suppose further that she and Richard do not have the stereotypical mother-in-law/son-in-law relationship that has provided fodder for many comedians and a good deal of work for many psychotherapists. Richard, having been an orphan, thinks of her as the mother he never had. The three of them enjoy each other's company and share many interests. They go to plays, rock concerts, antiques shows, and Sunday breakfasts together, especially now, after her husband has died. During the years that Richard and Pamela have been married, the three of them have lives full of love and caring for one another. Theirs is an adult and guilt-free relationship built upon mutual respect.

Given the preceding scenario, Harmon says that "the decision that the couple made is clean and straightforward: of course Mother can live out her days in the house she 'gave' them and even though it will be difficult, it's the right thing to do. The idea that Mother would live out the rest of her days among strangers is abhorrent to them."

## Making Assumptions

When Harmon imagines another set of facts, the "right thing to do" gets clouded. Suppose that Pamela's mother is a real shrew. Suppose further that she interferes in Pamela and Richard's lives at every opportunity. She constantly criticizes the housekeeping at her daughter's apartment and "plays favorites" with Pamela and Richard's children—even to the point of "forgetting" the last child's birthday for many years running. Suppose that holidays and family gatherings are cause for anxiety and depression, as in so many American homes, because the mother always criticizes Richard for not making enough money. She constantly reminds Richard about the rich boys whom Pamela had dated before and hints that she is going to leave all of her earthly possessions to the ASPCA because they take better care of the animals than Richard takes of Pamela and the kids. Suppose that, as the only child, Pamela was "Daddy's little girl," and Mother has always been jealous of the closeness they developed—and she lets Pamela know it. Suppose that Pamela drinks heavily as a result of not being able to grieve properly for her father and is not much able to take care of herself—much less take on the demands of caring for a person suffering with senile dementia. Suppose that Mother just gets more set in her ways as the dementia becomes more pronounced.

Where once she was just disagreeable, now she is unbearable. Suppose that Richard is the type of man who, because of an extreme sense of entitlement, has to play golf every day that the sun rises, and the bulk of the care would fall to Pamela. Suppose, further, that Richard and Pamela's marriage is not as strong as it could be and just one more little stressor will send Richard packing and Pamela into the abject poverty experienced by some divorced women. There she would be—drunk, abandoned, poor, burdened, and resentful.

"Given this scenario," Harmon says, "it is probably the wrong thing for them to move the mother into their house because she would be better off in a nursing home. At least strangers would not have a historical reason to be vengeful or to treat her shabbily."

## Independence: Important or Overrated?

I agree with Harmon in large measure. But I also want to provide a historical setting to their dilemma. Unlike with prior generations, in which there was always someone at home (often the wife, but sometimes an unmarried woman, the family spinster), many households today are empty during daylight hours. There is no one to watch out for frail, elderly parents, to pick them up when they fall, or simply to feed them when they forget to open a can of soup for themselves.

My concern is that in modern society, there is an unspoken assumption that the elderly are always better off living independently, away from their children. There is a sense of failure and shame attached to needing your own children for your care.

I don't share this view. I think family attachments and close, long-term relations are good things and ought to be promoted. I think that most elderly would be better off living with or near a family member. Perhaps they can't take care of themselves properly and they can't afford to pay for proper care. Or it may be that they are lonely; paid companionship doesn't substitute for friends or family.

Yet elderly parents moving in with their children isn't very popular. Americans prize our independence—treating it as a moral virtue—so that often neither parent nor child seriously considers living together. (The opposite side of the coin is equally true: many consider grown children choosing to live near their parents a sign of psychological immaturity, rather than an indication of strong family ties.) The elderly may feel guilty about imposing, they may feel ashamed of being dependent. They can't tolerate the role reversal, now having to rely on their children rather than vice versa. We often view dependence, for whatever reason, as a mark of failure. On the other side, the circumstances of the adult children often don't allow them to properly care for their parents. They may have to work, and not be able to be home with the parent, or to afford home care.

In this instance, the issue facing Richard and Pamela is not whether they think it is good for Pamela's mother to live with them (I assume the mother thinks it is) but how much of their own future they are willing to sacrifice in order to have her stay with them. Parents are expected to sacrifice quite a bit for the sake of their children. The needs of the children come first—paying for school, clothing, and so on before indulging in luxuries for themselves. It is the unethical parent who neglects his child. But how much is the child expected to sacrifice for the parent? That family members have obligations to one another is obvious. But not all obligations are of equal weight. Grown brothers and sisters have some obligation to care for one another, but not much, for example.

## Family Obligations

If there were a scale of family obligations, everything else being equal (a big assumption), those we have to our parents weigh more than those we have to our siblings but less than those we have to our spouses and our children. The advent of Social Security, pension plans, and so forth has lessened such obligations insofar as it has made the elderly financially independent. In Kenya, Nyangati and Ongesa's parents had to rely upon them. That's why the biblical commandment refers to the obligations of grown children to their elderly parents. The need isn't as acute today. My parents and my wife's parents could pay for their own apartments and food.

This means that the obligation we have to our elderly parents is voluntary, at least under certain circumstances. Someone who has been abandoned or abused by his parents has very little obligation to them, no more than the obligation toward strangers. But barring such situations, we are required to ensure that our parents live as long and as comfortably as possible. It is very much like the obligation we have to our own grown children.

Families are drawn together by ties that are more than what they can do for one another. The ideal is to have both economically independent elderly and grown children, who want to take care of their parents, even live with them. Family life, everything else being equal, is better than institutional life; being in a caring community is better than living alone.

## Actions Are More Important than Feelings

Children have a serious responsibility to make sure that their elderly parents are taken care of. It arises from the ethical principle of reciprocity—to return something to the person who has given you something. We don't have to particularly like our parents. We may never have chosen them as friends. But remember, the commandment tells us to honor our parents, not love them. Love is a sentiment, and feelings can't be conjured on command. We love one another as our hearts move us. Honor, though, is a set of actions, and behavior is subject to direction and is sustainable whatever one's emotional state. The honorable thing for grown children to do is at least to assure minimal care for elderly parents who cared for them, as a way of sustaining ties that make us more human.

Are Pamela and Richard sacrificing too much? If they are at risk of pauperizing themselves or seriously compromising the quality of their own lives, then they are paying too high a price. In that case there will be three helpless people, not one.

Having a parent move in isn't always the only ethical thing to do. As Harmon reminds us, "For many, obligation is built on fear: fear of emotional estrangement, fear of disinheritance, fear of responsibility. One strong figure can dominate the lives of so many others; and once that figure is gone, true feelings will emerge."

## The Limits of Obligation

There is yet another consideration here. This is Pamela's parent, not Richard's. Richard's obligation comes through his relationship with his wife. He may have competing obligations in his own family. What if he had an elderly parent of his own in a similar situation? Would it create resentment on the part of Richard's family, who might feel unfairly treated? Would this put a strain on the marriage? I know someone who would have brought his aging mother to live with them, except for the fact that both he and his wife worked and his wife couldn't justify it to her own mother, who was a jealous woman.

However, where the relationship is a decent one, where people respect one another, then I think that the sacrifice made is an ethically admirable one. If Richard and Pamela were to find the strain more than they could bear, there would be no shame in placing Pamela's mother in a home.

They are doing their best, and that is good.

# 17

# How Do I Know What Is Fair?

Karen is a single mother of three. Maria, ten, is a smart and talented but underachieving and petulant child. Greg, twelve, is a hardworking, sweet boy who needs little attention to remain an average student. Valerie, fourteen, was born with a debilitating chronic illness. Given constraints on her time, Karen has decided to divide her time equally among the three children.

Some questions to ask yourself:

1. What is fairness?
2. Is fairness the same as equality? As equity?
3. Which is more important, equality or equity?
4. Are fairness or equality useful concepts for a family to consider?
5. How do you decide which child should most benefit?
6. How do you measure benefit?
7. How do you decide which child should make the greatest sacrifice?
8. How do you measure harm?
9. Do you think Karen is doing the moral thing?

# The Problem:
# Choosing among Talent,
# Need, and Goodness

Karen's problem is impossibly difficult. It is a parent's bad dream. But as extreme as this situation appears, it is similar to what many parents face when making out a will. My wife and I had to think hard about what to do with our estate. We have two children, a foster daughter, and two grandchildren. How much money do we leave each child? Do we look at each child and decide who has the greatest need? Do we base our decision on whose lifestyle we most approve of and who will put the inheritance to best use? Do we treat the family as a unit, or each person as an individual? This last option isn't so much a problem as long as each family has an equal number of children. But what if this changes?

The opening vignette raises some of the most perplexing issues in all of moral philosophy. It pits three interests—that of the talented, the needy, and the average—against one another and asks us to decide what is the fair way to divide our time and resources. While posed in terms of domestic considerations, the issues it addresses apply to the larger world as well. A school board, for example, has a budget and must decide whether to spend its money on average students (the largest number), talented students (those who may make the largest contribution to society), or students with disabilities (who, per capita, are the most expensive to educate).

While Karen's dilemma is fictional, it is close to a real one I am familiar with. Jocelyn had three children—a girl, Stacey (not their real names), from her first, brief marriage, and two sons who were born in her second marriage. The daughter was a troubled child. Jocelyn loved her a great deal but no more than she loved her two sons. No matter what she did for her daughter, it was never enough.

Stacey was highly destructive to family life. She was abusive, stole from the family, and began to use drugs. Stacey took so much time, energy, and money away from the two boys that Jocelyn eventually forced her daughter out of the house. Jocelyn continued to love Stacey, but she felt that she couldn't sacrifice the lives of her two sons. Until her own death, Jocelyn felt guilty about excluding Stacey, but she was also convinced that she had done the right thing.

Every choice has it proponents and its critics.

# Those in Need:
# The Difference between
# Can't and Won't

Since biblical times people have been instructed to care for those in need, the orphaned and the widowed. But this can't mean all orphans and all widows. There's the old joke about a man who kills his parents and then asks mercy from the court because he is an orphan. Only a ludicrously strict reading of the injunction would move a court to such pity. The widow from a wealthy family who has no financial worries does not require special consideration in terms of money. If orphans and widows need special attention it is because, generally, they are vulnerable, particularly in traditional societies in which nearly all means of support are out of their control. When the husband and father dies, wives and children have to depend upon the goodwill of others for their survival.

This concept of caring for the needy has been extended over the centuries to include, among others, people who are poor, unemployed, and disabled. The question of how far to spread welfare and who is to be supported by it remains a difficult matter of public policy. Social policy debates over revamping New Deal and Great Society legislation have revolved around, at least in part, the following questions: Do you support all the poor or only the deserving poor? How do you define "deserving" and how do you determine if the person deserves society's support or not? Does making an effort count? What about those who can't make an effort, or is it the case that everyone can make an effort no matter how limited they may be? Who is handicapped, and how much does a society need to do in attempting to make the environment handicapped-accessible?

Knowing when someone is making a real effort is no easy matter. Sometimes I can't tell myself whether I am lazy or whether something else is interfering with my willpower. Once I was sick and didn't do much for about a week. I didn't know if this was because I didn't *feel* like working or because I wasn't *able* to work. The dividing lines among lack of motivation, physical enervation, and depression were blurred. Maybe I was using the illness as an excuse to get out of doing some unpleasant chores. Maybe I just wanted a good reason to get away from some responsibilities. Equally plausible was that the virus sapped me of my will and caused my lethargy. Occasionally a pep talk from my wife helped, but mainly nothing made a difference. For a week I was content to stay in bed, watching hours upon hours of television, which was very unlike me. Only when my illness was correctly diagnosed as Legionnaires' disease and treated did I return to myself.

If I couldn't tell the difference between "can't" and "won't" about myself, how nearly impossible is it to tell about another. But this is the kind of judgment we do make about those who depend upon us. And it is this sort of question that Karen in the story faces in an immediate way. Three people are relying upon her to varying degrees. She feels responsible for all and has responded to them by giving each an equal amount of time.

Karen could have reached her decision for one of two reasons: out of sheer despair in trying to find a better way to handle the demands on her, or a belief that fairness means absolute equality.

From one point of view, an equal division of time among all concerned is unfair. For example, Karen probably would not think that the best way to feed her family is by giving each an equal portion of food. Some people need to eat more than others, some have higher metabolism rates. Likewise, she may also choose to reward one with a treat because he or she helped in a special way. It is unfair to treat people differently for arbitrary reasons, such as simple dislike, but there may well be good reasons to treat people differently as a matter of fairness.

## Merit: What a Person Deserves

One way to analyze Karen's decision is to distinguish between *need* and *merit*. All three need Karen but for different reasons. All children need a parent's attention and affection. These children, however, are different from one another. Maria is intelligent and talented. She is also a pain in the neck. I guess that if you ask Maria what she wants from her mother, she might say, "To be left alone." However, Karen shouldn't give Maria only what she wants, for it may not be in her daughter's interests in the long run. Besides, wants are complex, especially for an almost-teenager. If Karen were to leave her alone, Maria's talents may remain dormant. This would be unfair to the Maria who isn't yet the adult Maria-to-be. Maria's real need, therefore, is to be encouraged, coaxed, and cajoled by her mother, to be supported to overcome her petulance and develop both her mind and her talents. She deserves Karen's attention not because she merits it based upon what she does but because of who she is—that is, Karen's daughter.

Greg is a likable kid. He is hardworking but lacks Maria's abilities, and his school grades are mediocre. His mother's encouragement wouldn't make much of a difference. He simply lacks his sister's potential. Maria's ability, however, is latent. By objective measurements used in school, Greg surpasses his sister. But no matter how hard his mother works with him, he will never be more than an average student. However, neglecting him isn't an ethical choice, since he is as deserving as Maria, for the same reason—mainly, that he is Karen's child. At the same time, one could say he deserves more from Karen than does Maria because his efforts should be rewarded. That would mean giving less to Maria.

There is another child in this family. Valerie is disabled. She didn't cause her condition. She doesn't deserve her lot. She is a victim of circumstances. If she doesn't receive extraordinary attention, she will always have something less than a full life. However, to give her what she needs to reach an acceptable level means taking something away from the other two children, who are deserving in their own right.

## Merit: The Relationship to Being Good

If Karen were to give her children attention based upon personal likes and dislikes, she probably would give the least to Maria. Maria is, after all, a difficult child. Greg, on the other hand, is earnest, and Valerie can't help but elicit a strong sense of sympathy. If Karen were to give more attention to the one who could make the most use of it, it would probably be Maria, since the extra effort is likely to lead to greater results. Maria, after all, has untapped talent and intelligence. In so doing, Karen would be penalizing Greg, since he would lose his mother's attention relative to his sister through no fault of his own. Valerie also would suffer.

This vignette echoes the parable of the prodigal son found in the Christian Bible. In this story, an older son leaves home upon receiving his share of his father's property. Through foolish spending and debauchery, he becomes penniless. Repenting his ways, he returns to his father's home, asking forgiveness. His father gives him a robe, a ring, and shoes, and slaughters a sheep on his behalf. The younger son, seeing this, becomes angry, since he has remained loyal to his father. He complains that despite his steadfastness, he has never received such treatment from his father. The father answers by explaining that the younger son has always been with him but the older was as good as dead but now is alive again.

The parable stands for God's forgiveness of sinners. But from a moral point of view, it is questionable. It seems to say that those who are a constant can be taken for granted; those who stray and return will be showered with love. Why should Greg lose his mother's attention because Maria is indolent? At the same time, Maria may have a greater need for her mother's attention. She may have a greater psychological need than Greg—be more unsure of herself, more confused, more vulnerable. There is no way to know without understanding more of the history and dynamics of the family life.

Greg deserves more of Karen's attention if merit is measured by being a good person. Maria deserves more of Karen's attention if merit is measured in terms of potentialities. And Valerie deserves the most attention if merit is measured in terms of need. Greg is now getting enough from his mother, but Maria could use more. Maria, therefore, is needier than Greg. But Greg's needs may grow if time is diverted to his sister. Like the elder son in the biblical parable, Greg may turn resentful. To mollify his hurt feelings, Karen would then have to turn her attention once more to her son.

What moral guidance can anyone give Karen? I'm not sure. She is faced with a Sophie's choice: one child has to be sacrificed to save another. Given these complexities, Karen's decision is a fair one, although mechanical. Love, affection, and care can't be toted up as in a ledger. But time is an objective measure by which she can keep herself on track. Although she may do better if she concerns herself less with the clock, it does provide her with a helpful structure. The claims of equality and considerations of need and merit are difficult matters both conceptually and practically. Philosophers, politicians, and social scientists struggle with them. Karen's solution, I believe, is fair. Other decisions are possible and could also be viewed as fair. What makes this anecdote so difficult is that each of the three competing claims is legitimate and each in its own right demands consideration.

# Culture:
## Two Ways of Understanding Fairness

Consider a 1983 study of traditional and modern healers among the Akamba in East Africa. They were presented with this question: To which patient should a doctor give the scarce life-saving medicine when faced with two critical patients but only enough medicine to save one? The Akambas tended to respond that they would divide the medicine equally, risking death for both patients, rather than give one privilege over the other.

This decision is different from the one that most Americans would make. In 1993, conjoined twins Angela and Amy Lakeberg, both attached breast to belly, shared one liver and one heart. There was no chance of survival for either if they remained in the conjoined state. Their parents decided to save one at the expense of the other. At Children's Hospital in Philadelphia, surgeons deliberately cut off circulation to Amy to salvage the heart for Angela. British courts reached a similar decision in 2000, over the protests of the parents, who didn't want the twins separated because it meant the inevitable death of one, even though not having the operation would be the death of both. The court said it boldly: to save one child, the doctors had to kill another.

While usually something cannot be both right and not right at the same time, I think the American and Akamba ways of looking at the matter of fairness are both correct. There is no rational way to choose one over the other. They are two ways of understanding fairness and they are both correct, even though they lead to different actions. The differences turn on cultural, not moral, choices. Or more accurately, the values of a culture highlight one kind of fairness over another.

John Mbiti, a theologian from Kenya and a former visiting professor of world religions at Princeton University, refused to discuss Karen's situation as a moral issue.

"I question whether it is right to turn the life of Karen and her children into an ethical problem, hanging between right and wrong. Does she consider her action, her decision, and her life with the children to pose an ethical situation? What about her children? Is it fair to look at them as posing an ethical problem for their mother? How would they feel about that if they knew that they were so regarded by society? I do not feel comfortable about discussing Karen and her family as an ethical problem. This isn't a question of right or wrong. It is a family situation, which requires such action on the part of the mother. At times, the illness would necessitate more attention than at others. Valerie and Karen, as well as other children, grow into such a routine of life, accept it, and live with it."

Mbiti accepts Karen's approach. He says, "Each of her children needs her time. It is right and proper that she shares it on an equal basis." But Mbiti also says that "this need not be done mechanically: at times, one or the other child will need extra time from her. At times, Karen will spend time with the children collectively as a group. Far more important is the content of that shared resource. The content—that is, what she does with the children (individually or together)—has more value than just the mathematical sharing of time. The children, whatever their individual situations may be, are growing up. Changes will come upon the children. Their needs will also change. Karen's time for them will have to be adjusted accordingly."

## Love and Care: Are These Fairness?

Mbiti and I both agree that, as he says, "the intensity of her love and care, the attention and recognition she gives to each child, the encouragement and hope she instills in each child, the self-confidence she helps grow in each child, the trust she builds in each child have to be cultivated and nourished, and in the long run, it may not matter whether Karen divides her time 'equally' among her children. It is these values that may last longer and give a deeper support to the children than merely the mathematical portions of passing time."

Assuming all this to be true about Karen, she still has to make a decision, and the one she has made is for absolute equality. Some things don't have a perfect solution or even a good solution. So we do the best we can. As long as a concern for fairness and loving care are at the root of her decision, it is an ethical decision, no matter the type of fairness that she chooses.

# PART FOUR

## Ethics in the World

# 18

❧

# How Long Must
# I Keep a Promise?

Martha was an ardent supporter of the civil rights movement. During a student protest, a Ku Klux Klan member permanently disabled a young activist, Florence. Martha, who hadn't participated in the sit-in herself, pledged to support the injured woman for the rest of her life. For more than forty years she has sent her a monthly check. Martha is now retired and lives on a fixed income.

Martha has examined her expenses and has decided to stop the monthly stipend to the woman she never met.

Some questions to ask yourself:

1. What makes a promise binding?
2. Is a promise to an unmet stranger different from other types of promises?
3. Are there any circumstances under which a promise can be broken?
4. Are there time limits on promises?
5. Is Martha doing the moral thing by stopping the payment?

# The Problem:
# Keeping Our Word
# When Circumstances Change

Humans can survive only if we can count on one another. That's why we have the saying, a person is only as good as his word. The saying makes explicit that "goodness" and dependability go hand in hand. Moral character is inseparable from keeping promises.

What we say to another matters. We expect that what we are told will be more or less close to the truth. A legal contract is binding only if the facts are represented accurately. Indeed, the first U.S. diplomatic treaty signed under the Constitution, with the Iroquois Confederacy in 1794, is still in force. Each year the U.S. government delivers $4,500 worth of cloth to the Iroquois.

In the ethical world, promises tend to be more open-ended. Promises aren't full of stipulations. We assume goodwill on the part of the person making the promise. And often there are major assumptions about the promise that may or may not be shared by both parties.

## Serious and Trivial Promises

Throughout our lives we make many promises, some thoughtful, some offhanded, some serious, and some casual. Old acquaintances meet on the street, strike up a conversation, and part promising to call one another. This is the sort of promise that is more a social convention than an untruth. Some of our promises are not meant to carry much weight. We call them promises but they are more like an intent. "Maybe I'll call," is what we really mean to say. "I'll give it some thought, and if I feel like rekindling our ties, I'll call you."

Hurt arises if one of the parties takes the promise literally and feels rejected when future contact is spurned. But this is the way we conduct much of our social lives. We often say these things not to deceive others but to spare their feelings—and our own. Social lies keep us from saying to another, "You know, I'm glad we haven't seen each other in years. And I have absolutely no interest in ever seeing you again." The enactment of the little charade is harmless as long as everyone understands the no one is to be held to the literalness of the words.

What makes a promise a real promise is not that we utter the words, but that there is a serious aim behind the utterance and the party who hears it believes that it is meant to be serious. A promise is a verbal social contract. To breach a commercial contract is serious. We can be sued; we can go to jail. Courts assess damages and we must pay. But breaking a promise doesn't have consequences of this kind. The breach is not legal, but social; the damages assessed are exacted by those in our web of relationships. The similarity between contracts and promises is that in both there is an obligation to fulfill an expectation. In the case of contracts, the expectation is spelled out in writing. In the case of promises, the expectation is spoken. But contracts and promises are important in law and ethics because they are instruments that enable us to count on each other. We depend upon the enforcement of contracts and promises because we understand that it is a source of dependability and social cohesion. If promises were not meant to be fulfilled, if they weren't serious obligations, we would live in a society in which no one's word meant anything.

## Why It's Important to Keep Promises

Trying to live well in a society in which keeping one's word is the exception would be next to impossible. Nothing could get done, since we could never coordinate our activities, never know if what we were told was in fact the case. If we didn't trust a person's word, we would not be able to rely on her. If we were not obliged to fulfill the promises we made, then in effect, we would be lying. We would be saying something that we did not mean. Promises are important because we believe in the intentions of the person making the promises. The belief rests on our sense that when a promise is made there is an obligation to fulfill it, and the acquittal of that obligation should not be made casually or unilaterally.

Promises are important because they help to protect the vulnerable. Lying and breaking promises are both forms of power over the unsuspecting. When a promise is made, the other person comes to rely upon it. As a promise reduces uncertainty, the person who is counting on the promise being met becomes vulnerable because her guard is down, she makes no contingent plans. She is counting on something that she rightly expects to receive. It makes a difference to her that the other person honestly tries to do what she promised. Whatever the content is of a particular promise, the implicit promise is, "I will not take advantage of you; I will not harm you."

Because breaking a promise can do harm, keeping promises is high on the list of what it means to be ethical. This is why breaking a promise is so difficult for the person who thinks of herself as ethical. Not to honor a promise is dishonest; it also hurts another. The person most let down is one's self. Promise-keeping goes to the heart of self-esteem, whereas promise-breaking is an attack upon one's integrity.

Yet there are times when fulfilling a promise is not a moral duty, as in the example about promising to call someone you haven't seen in a while. If it makes no difference to anyone whether it is fulfilled, then there is no reason for honoring it. Another reason for breaking a promise might be that meeting it would cause a greater harm. Still another reason for not fulfilling a promise is that the conditions under which the promise was made have so changed that it is no longer reasonable to expect that the promise must be kept.

So while the obligation to keep one's promise is strict, it is not the only consideration. Occasionally something else carries greater weight.

## Good Reasons to Keep or Break a Promise

There are several factual points about Martha's pledge and her decision to renege that should be considered: one, she made the pledge voluntarily; two, she made it to aid someone who needed financial assistance; three, the recipient needed the pension because she made a sacrifice for a cause that Martha also supported; four, the pledge was made long ago; and five, Martha's financial condition has changed.

The voluntary nature of the pledge is important. If Martha had been forced or tricked into making it, that would be a different matter. Or if she didn't know what she was doing or did it impulsively, that would also alter the situation somewhat. But Martha seemed to know very well what she was doing.

The promise was for something important. Martha believed in the cause she was supporting. It's possible that if she could have gone herself to protest, she would have. For whatever reason, she didn't, and she decided to support the cause through a monetary pledge. If the promise was made for a trivial reason for a trivial cause, then the bonds holding Martha to her word wouldn't be very strong. But here we are dealing with significant matters of justice and even permanent damage to someone's physical capacities.

The receiver of the pledge continues to need Martha's support. Although the promise was made long ago, Martha intended for the pledge to be permanent since Florence's disability was permanent. If Florence no longer depended on money from Martha, then the situation would be different.

The promise was made decades ago. Many things have changed in more than thirty years. Circumstances change with the times, and time does lessen the strength of the promise. But time alone doesn't loosen the bond completely.

The circumstances of the person who made the promise have changed. The question here is how much Martha's finances have changed. If they have altered so much that Martha is, in essence, no longer the same person who made the promise, then the promise isn't binding.

## Weighing Costs and Benefits

I wondered if a moral philosopher would be helpful in thinking about Martha's situation. Peter Singer, who is a professor of bioethics at Princeton University's Center for Human Values, believes that since moral philosophers spend their time thinking about moral arguments, they can be helpful where the facts are reasonably clear. So I asked him what he thought about Martha.

Singer says, "My view is that Martha ought to try to find out what the financial circumstances of the disabled person are. If the hardship that she would herself be experiencing by continuing to send the money is greater than, or comparable to, the hardship that the recipient would suffer by no longer getting the money, she is not obliged to keep sending it. After thirty years, she has fulfilled her obligations as well as anyone can reasonably expect, in fact better than that, and I don't think she should feel bound to continue it, unless it will cause significantly greater net hardship to stop it."

Finding out the real conditions for Florence is important. This seems the right time for Martha to take such a step. Just as Martha extended her sympathy to a woman she never met, Martha may be surprised to find that Florence will extend understanding toward her. That's the hope, anyway. It is also possible that Florence is an embittered and nasty person who feels entitled to the subsidy she has received for years.

I disagree with Singer in his adding up a ledger of benefits and costs as a way of reaching a decision about Martha's moral problem. When countries sign a treaty, the treaty cannot be broken because the ledger sheets, as calculated by one side or the other, no longer add up the way they did on the day it was signed. Sometimes we make promises expecting one outcome, but find that things turn in unexpected ways. In some ways, a promise is like a bet. It is taking a chance on the future, and no one knows what the future will bring. If promises remained in force only when it suited us individually, this would hardly bring with it the kind of assurance that promises are intended to create.

## Very Good Reasons to Keep a Promise

Martha's promise was a serious one, and another person has come to depend upon her fulfilling that financial pledge. If she is to break the promise, there must be a strong, overriding reason. Martha's reason is that to continue to assist the activist is to put herself in financial straits. She made her pledge many years ago, when her life still lay in its fullness before her. Now she is a nearly an old woman herself. At an earlier age she could accommodate the activist's pension as part of her budget. This, evidently, is no longer the case. The young Martha was who made the promise couldn't reasonably have been expected to imagine what her life would be like a half century later. She may not have even thought so far ahead.

Perhaps Martha was foolish in making such a sweeping pledge. But she did. Her present-day self is bound by a decision of her young self. Nevertheless, if that promise would now cause her serious harm, she need not be strictly held to it. While it would be wrong for her to precipitously cut off her aid, she could inform Florence about her changed circumstances, inquire about the extent to which Florence still needs money, attempt to raise funds elsewhere for her, and begin to reduce her payments.

Whether Martha is morally correct in stopping payment depends upon whether she truly needs the money for her own well-being. In this instance, Martha's well-being must be defined in essentials, not luxuries. If she were to fall ill because she didn't have money for her own medical care, that is one thing. If it means forgoing a movie, that is another. However, only Martha can determine the essentials of her life. Going to the movie may be one of the few things Martha does that brings joy to her life, and living a happy life is a goal shared by every rational being.

If Martha stops her payments, it shouldn't be because they are an inconvenience or that Martha has changed her mind. The only way her obligation is overridden is if in carrying it out, she would endanger her own well-being.

# 19

## Can the Ends Justify the Means I Use?

A convicted mobster decides to make a charitable contribution. He offers more than $1 million to a hospital to build a children's wing. He will make the contribution if the new pavilion is named after him. The hospital board accepts the gift, with that stipulation.

Some questions to ask yourself:

1. Who is hurt if the hospital turns down the money?
2. Who will benefit if the money is accepted?
3. Do you think that the source of a gift matters?
4. Does the motivation behind a gift matter?
5. What is the responsibility of the board of a nonprofit organization?
6. Would it be different if the donor's name wasn't on the building?
7. Does the size of the gift make a difference?
8. Do you think the hospital is right in accepting the gift?

# The Problem:
# Doing Good with
# Something Obtained Immorally

The conflict in this story is between the hospital's need for the money and the money's being tainted and coming with a controversial string attached. Nonprofit organizations engage in situations like this all the time. You can probably name a religious institution that has put the name of a morally questionable person on a plaque, or a university that has offered an honorary degree to a celebrity, or a city that has named a stadium after a corporate donor. At the university in which I teach, there is a modest building named after a prominent political figure who served a year in a federal prison for extorting money for his political party from county employees. And in recent years, many nonprofit groups have engaged in land deals that have been criticized by environmental organizations. The John D. and Catherine T. MacArthur Foundation, the "genius granting" foundation, faced this problem with its investment in Florida property. Murray Gell-Mann, a Nobel Prize winner on the MacArthur board, asked, "Do you make a financial sacrifice for local environmental reasons and then make it less easy to make grants for worthy causes, including important environmental causes elsewhere?"

# Understanding the Reasons
# of Various Parties Involved

Matters of this sort raise questions about the public good. The answer therefore should evolve out of a public discussion, one that promotes communication among the various parties involved. Where do we draw the line? How do we draw the line? I asked a journalist what he thought. Rick Seifert was part of a team that won a Pulitzer Prize for its reporting on the Mount St. Helens eruption and its aftermath. He also published a community newspaper in Portland, Oregon. Seifert says that as a journalist his job is to lay out the issues involved and attempt to understand the perspectives and interests of the people involved—in this case the mobster's, the hospital board's, the children who will need the hospital facilities, the community as a whole. He says that the question lurking behind the story is this: "Did the hospital's decision go beyond some benchmark of a community standard of acceptable behavior?"

As with many ethical problems, it's useful to get as many facts as possible. Here are the people Seifert would interview and some of the questions he would ask as a journalist:

*The chair of the hospital board.* How large was the majority in favor of this decision? Were other potential benefactors approached and what were their responses? Was the decision forced because without this money there would be no new wing? Was the board approached or did it solicit this donation? How do you respond to the criticism that the money is "ill-gotten" gains? How do you think the public will react? Did the board discuss possible public reaction, and if so, what did they imagine it to be?

*A dissenting board member, if any.* Why did you oppose the decision? Would the gift have been acceptable without the name condition? What does the decision say about our values today? Do you feel the board majority is in tune with community values?

*The mobster.* Why did you decide to give to the hospital? Did you initiate the idea of the gift? Why was the name provision made a requirement of the gift? What is the source of this money? Did it come from legitimate businesses? What do you feel the public's reaction will be to your gift and to the name provision? Were you surprised that the board accepted? Have other donations from you been refused or accepted, and if so, by whom? (If others refused or accepted, they would be interviewed.) Do you feel remorse for what you have done? Is this contribution a form of restitution?

*The chief of the medical staff.* Will the board's decision affect the medical mission of the hospital? Do you agree with the decision?

*A sampling of parents with children who would benefit from the new wing.* What are your reactions to the decision?

*Public officials.* What are your reactions to the decision? Would you have accepted such a gift for a public building? A library or courthouse, for instance?

*Health maintenance organization officials* who might refer patients to the hospital. Will this decision affect your patronage and referrals to the hospital?

*A professor of ethics* from a local college or university. What does the decision say about the ethics of the board and its sense of the ethics of the community? How do you analyze this decision ethically?

*A religious leader,* particularly if the hospital is a sectarian one. Would your church or synagogue accept such a gift?

*Hospital volunteers.* Does the acceptance of the gift change your feelings about the hospital and its leadership?

*The leader of another public service institution.* What would you do if you were in the same position as the hospital's leadership?

# The Importance of Benevolence

These are all good questions and go into deciding whether the hospital's action was morally justifiable. But the facts also should be filtered through some general principles regarding the uses and abuses of money, and the relationship between means and ends. It also presents a problem of proportionality. What I mean is how much bad is done in the cause of doing how much good.

First, some general observations about giving money. There is near unanimity among religious leaders and moral philosophers that the accumulation of money isn't a good in itself but that money should be used to help those most in need. Parting with one's wealth is endorsed by every religion. The Hindu Rig-Veda says, "The wealthier man should give to the needy"; the Jewish Bible reminds us that "He who gives to the poor shall not lack"; the New Testament states, "It is more blessed to give than to receive"; and giving alms to the poor is one of the five pillars of the Muslim faith. Similar sentiments are found in other religious and ethical traditions. The wealthy are implored to part with a portion of their wealth to support those in need. Modern society forces people to be charitable by taxing them, so as to redistribute their wealth to underwrite community needs and support the less fortunate.

# Making the Best of a Bad Situation

But what do we do with the money that has been gotten unethically or illegally? There is a story told about a minister in Pennsylvania years ago. One of his parishioners, Jack, enjoyed fishing more than churchgoing. One Monday morning he presented the minister with several pickerels. The minister thanked Jack for the gift.

"But those fish were caught yesterday," Jack said. "Perhaps your conscience won't let you eat them."

The parson stretched out his hand to take the fish. "There's one thing I know. The pickerel weren't to blame."

The tax collector has much the same attitude. Al Capone was imprisoned for tax evasion, after all.

There are numerous examples of something good having come out of, if not dirty money, then "gray" money. For example, the world's most prestigious peace prize carries the name of the inventor of nitroglycerine and dynamite. Evidently prodded by a guilty conscience, Alfred Nobel, one of the richest men in the world, upon his death left his entire fortune to reward "those persons who shall contribute most materially to benefiting mankind during the year immediately preceding." In 1997, the money from the dynamite fortune was used to fund a group whose mission it was to remove land mines from around the world.

Nineteenth-century robber barons present another example. During most of his life, Andrew Carnegie was the embodiment of the "gospel of wealth." This doctrine included the least public interference with individualism, private property, and the process of accumulation. However, for the last two decades of his life, Carnegie turned the tables on himself and became the paragon of philanthropy. During his lifetime he financed more than 2,500 public libraries and gave away more than $300 million to numerous good causes. Thousands of poor children were able to read books because of Carnegie's gift. Today Carnegie and others like him stand as models of selfless use of money.

Whether the Nobels and Carnegies made their fortunes honorably is arguable. In regard to the vignette presented here, there is no question about the origins of the money. The donor is a convicted mobster and the money is tainted. Now he wants to take his money and wash it by putting it to a socially acceptable purpose. The temptation to take it is great. Look at all the good that has come from ethically questionable philanthropists—libraries, museums, and concert halls. If this mobster wants to put his money into helping children, then let him. Take the money, put his name on the hospital, and use the money to treat sick children, even save their lives in many instances.

## How Much Harm versus How Much Good

Whether to accept the money is similar to some of the questions considered by institutional review boards at hospitals. I once served on such a committee at Long Island Jewish Hospital, a major research center. The task of this group was to pass on the ethical acceptability of research. The ethical consideration behind many of the requests for research was the relationship between means and ends. All the proposals intended to improve the medical treatment of illness, but was the method proposed by the researcher consistent with ethical principles, whatever the desired outcome?

Each month I received a packet of proposals, sent my recommendations to the chair, then later in the month discussed these and other proposals with the entire committee. As one of the lay members, I wasn't being asked to comment on the validity of the research (that was done by peer review) but on the ethics of the protocol. Mostly we wanted to ensure that the patient had given his informed consent. Did he give his consent voluntarily, did he understand the risks involved? Did he understand the nature of the research? Occasionally the morality of the research turned on whether the protocol stepped over an ethical boundary: Did the possible side effects outweigh the potential gains, did the research subject the volunteer to such risk that it should not even be attempted? Most proposals were routine, only minor changes such as requiring the language to be put in plain English. Occasionally a protocol was rejected.

Once, we turned down a psychiatrist's proposal to study the causes of panic attacks because his experiment would deliberately bring on the symptoms he wanted to study. In effect, the committee said that no one can volunteer to be tortured, even if the results of the experiment would be a real benefit to sufferers of such disorders.

Today all research involving human subjects, whether at a hospital or at a university, even if it involves something as innocuous as a questionnaire, must be approved by an ethics committee. Not so in the past. Experiments secretly done on black men to determine the effects of syphilis is one not so distant example from the United States of unethical research.

## Will Using Something Bad Encourage Others to Do Bad Things?

Another example comes from the Second World War. Upon entering Dachau, Allied troops found documents detailing the results of medical experiments performed by Nazi doctors upon living and unwilling prisoners. How much pain could a person stand? What were the sources of pain? How did people react to particular vaccines? The results of those experiments are still under seal. The medical profession refuses to look at the material contained in the files because the method used in obtaining it was unethical. The position is that publishing the information obtained from the experiments upon humans would condone the methods employed by the German doctors. It would be a triumph of the ultimate utilitarian ethic—the ends justifying the most depraved means. Furthermore, the fear is that if the now-sealed studies were published, it would open the door to other unscrupulous human experiments.* This is a variation of the "slippery slope" argument often used in ethics. Once you slide down the questionable ethical terrain, there is no stopping or controlling what happens next.

There is a case to be made, though, for the release of the data contained in those files. Information there may turn out to be useful in curing certain illnesses. The psychiatrist at the Long Island hospital may not have to design a new study to find out the cause of panic attacks; maybe the answer is already waiting to be read. As it is now, the information in the Nazi files does no one any good. Since the information already exists (and may never be gotten in any other way), let it help others. We can't undo the torture or bring the dead back to life. But if we did read the records, the victims of the experiments would be honored—their deaths would not have been in vain. Listening to this line of reasoning, a friend of mine scornfully said you could call the repository of such information the Joseph Mengele Institute for Anatomical Studies.

## Short-Term Consequences

Seifert believes that in the situation of the hospital, the board's decision cries out for public comment and discussion. The board would have to make an exceedingly compelling case in support of its actions or there would have to be equally compelling extenuating circumstances.

What might those circumstances be? Seifert asks, "Has the donor paid his debt to society by serving out a prison term? Is he

---

* Evidently, the American military in the Pacific had different ethical sensibilities from those in Europe. According to Iris Chang, author of *The Rape of Nanking*, the United States exonerated Japanese doctors who had engaged in diabolical medical experiments in exchange for their data about the effects of germ and biological weapons.

rehabilitated? What was the nature of his crime? How long ago did it happen? Has he expressed remorse about his former life? Did the donation come from legitimate activities he engaged in after his rehabilitation? Is he now a respected member of the community in his own right?"

The problem with accepting the money is that while it may make children healthier and even save lives, the hospital would be endorsing and even honoring criminal behavior.

But won't children suffer who would otherwise not if the gift is rejected? Yes. Fewer will be treated as well as they could if there were a new and better facility. But—and this is the convincing argument for me—if money could buy respectability, if fortunes could clear the names of people who are otherwise contemptible, then all ethical standards and values amount to nothing more than talk. This is sometimes the case, where money talks and might makes right—clichés that reflect social reality. But saying that it happens all the time doesn't make it right. A description isn't the same as a prescription, and ethics is about prescribing the right moral course. Sociology describes what *does* happen but ethics portrays what *ought* to happen.

Seifert takes a step back from the immediate situation and comments that "it says something about our community that the board would feel compelled to take money from a mobster. Why weren't others in the community willing to step forward? Is the community so impoverished that there simply aren't other sources of funds?"

## The Long-Term Harm
## May Be Too High

Good questions, and Seifert is correct in broadening the focus. Nevertheless, the hospital board had to make a decision when the gift was offered. Lobbying for funds and launching a public relations campaign are long-term strategies. Faced with the choice it has to make, the hospital board could—and I think should—turn down the gift. By accepting it, they become complicit in how the money was gotten and condone all such future behavior. The gift surely would aid children, but at the same time it would help make gangsters who violate the social order equal to doctors who toil to make the world a better place.

It is possible that the gangster has seen the errors of his ways and now wants to become a respectable citizen by putting his money to good use. Sainthood is always an option for the sinful, but this hardly seems the case here, because he wants his name prominently displayed. Henry Ward Beecher once said, "A man should fear when he enjoys only the good he does publicly. Is it not publicity rather than charity, which he loves?" This is an echo of the thoughts of the twelfth-century Jewish philosopher Maimonides, who created a hierarchy of giving and placed anonymous charity at the top of the list. So if the mobster were sincere, he wouldn't attach any strings—no name, nothing. There is no change of heart if he insists upon putting his name on the institution.

But it isn't his heart that matters but the money, the counter-argument goes. True, but if the money comes from his crimes, then it really isn't even his to give away. He has no claim to it and he has no right to the fame that comes from donating someone else's money. Here I have to make an assumption. Since the protagonist is identified as a convicted mobster and he has $1 million to give away, he isn't a petty thief. And the gravity of his offense makes a difference in the decision whether to accept the money. As with the Nazi doctors, their crimes were crimes against humanity and there should be no question that memories of their deeds should only be ones of opprobrium.

So I agree with Seifert. I don't think the hospital should take the money from someone who is a morally corrupt, no matter how useful that money may be.

# 20

❦

# Is It Ever Right for Me to Discriminate?

Sally is looking for a new secretary. She interviews several people, all of whom are competent. She decides to offer the job to Tisha, even though Tisha does not type as fast or have as much prior experience as the other candidates, because Tisha is African American.

Some questions to ask yourself:

1. Should a position always go to the best-qualified person?
2. Should you take into account someone's personal condition when offering a job?
3. How do you determine who is best qualified?
4. Should factors other than skill be taken into account when giving someone a job?
5. Are preferences based on race, gender, or ethnicity always wrong?
6. Is it fair to penalize people for wrongs done in the past?
7. Is Sally's action moral?

# The Problem:
# An Individual versus
# a Member of a Group

Sally has placed herself directly in the thicket of the controversy surrounding affirmative action/reverse discrimination by giving the job to Tisha not because she is the best-qualified person but because of her race. Another way of saying this is that Sally does not give the job to others because they are white. This violates a basic ethical value, namely, no one should be discriminated against on the basis of their color. Assuming that Sally is well-meaning, what is her thinking? Can she justify her actions in the court of moral judgment?

Affirmative action generally refers to policies by government and other institutions, such as schools, that give preference to members of racial or ethnic groups and women. In this example, Sally's decision is beyond the scope of the typical debate, since she is simply using her own discretion rather than enforcing policies or regulations. Nevertheless, her actions favor Tisha because of her race and in that way are very much like government programs that some criticize as convoluted, confusing, and divisive. The morally correct position, the critics of affirmative action claim, is racially neutral, treating every person as an individual, not a member of a particular group of people.

The question around the ethics of affirmative action comes down to this: Should everyone be treated equally, as an individual whose competence is the only relevant consideration, or are there circumstances in which people should not be treated alike as individuals, but responded to as representatives of a class of people?

Sally's argument is that some people need a break more than

others because of their background. Preferences need to be given to some because of past injustices. Fairness must take into consideration historical and political realities. Sally's giving special consideration to Tisha because of past injustices, therefore, is the morally correct thing to do.

## People Should Be Judged as Individuals

Those opposed to Sally's argument say that preferences run counter to the principle of equality and that impartiality should always trump partiality. The prime ethical principle is simple: All people should be treated equally. Fairness requires that people be "color blind." By choosing Tisha over others because of her race, Sally discriminates against others because of their race. Sally's actions, therefore, are immoral.

One of the strongest opponents of affirmative action is Supreme Court justice Clarence Thomas. In an opinion in 1989, he declared that there is "moral and constitutional equivalence" between laws promoting affirmative action and those supporting slavery. They are both wrong, he wrote, because they treat people not as individuals but as members of a class. Thomas argued that the fairest way for society to reward people is to treat each as an individual, with the only important factor being how well the person performs. Factors such as history, race, or ethnicity should be bracketed by society, counting for nothing in determining who gets what. If there are a limited number of positions available, the slots go to those who have the highest grades, work most efficiently, are the strongest, and so forth. If one hundred positions are open for the freshman class, the hundred with the highest SATs and grade averages should be admitted.

Ward Connerly, the successful leader of the fight in California against affirmative action, who himself is black, writes, "When we become citizens of this nation, at birth or otherwise, we get a warranty with our citizenship. We are guaranteed the right to vote, the right to due process, the right to be a free people and not to be held as slaves, and the right to equal treatment under the law, regardless of our race, color, national origin, sex or ethnic background. . . . At the core of the American spirit is a sense of fair play. About thirty years ago, we embraced the concept of affirmative action to remedy the harm that had been done to black people."

What was intended to be a temporary solution to give blacks equal opportunity, Connerly says, has been transformed into a system that applies different standards to different individuals in order to create parity between racial groups. "What we found morally wrong and defined as discrimination thirty years ago," he writes, "we now simply ignore when it [affects] white males or Asians or someone else whose group has more than its statistical share of the public pie."

From this point of view, Sally in our example is being unfair to all those she rejects who are more qualified that Tisha. In making her decision, Sally may be taking a historical view, one in which citizens have an obligation to pay for past harms condoned by society. But should present-day job seekers be penalized for something done in the past? Representative Henry Hyde doesn't think so. He said, "The notion of collective guilt for what people did [over] 200 years ago, that this generation should pay a debt for that generation, is an idea whose time has gone. I never owned a slave. I never oppressed anybody. I don't know that I should have to pay for someone who did [own slaves] generations before I was born." A letter writer to the *Washington Post* answered Hyde by writing, "Well, because some people are descendants of slave owners and have profited from the labor of blacks who were never paid for their labor."

# Having Standards to Meet Particular Needs

The anti-affirmative action argument contends that society should allocate its resources much as winners are rewarded in an athletic competition. The event is won by the fastest, not the favorite. At least that is the theory behind competitive judging.

In fact, sometimes even sporting events aren't and can't be judged simply on objective criteria. Some events lend themselves to objective measurements—who jumped the highest, lifted the heaviest weight, crossed the finish line with the fastest time—but the same isn't true for sports that have a subjective element in the scoring. That is why there are several judges in figure skating. Form is an aesthetic element, something that appeals to the senses, or the sense of pleasure, or the eye of the judge.

If scoring were completely objective, we would need only one judge, or even better, a machine. Skating (and judging) is as much an art as a science, however, and each judge sees something slightly different. Therefore, it may not, in some totally objective sense, be the skater who is the *best* who has won, but the skater whom a particular set of judges has deemed to be the best. Most of the time, that subjective side to scoring is kept in check by the desire of the judges to be fair. But anyone who has watched competitive ice dancing knows that, for example, Canadian judges favor Canadians, American judges lean a little toward American skaters, and so forth.

The subjective element need not be biased against any one individual, although it may be. Superstars in basketball get away with much more than do rookies. The NBA is a business, and its economic success turns on fans cheering the future Hall of Famers. So we don't want the greats sitting on the bench because of fouls. The result is that the refs, in fact, have different standards for different players, depending upon their popularity. Another example, this time from baseball: Three umpires are discussing the nature of the strike, a notoriously elusive dimension. The first ump says he calls them as they are. The second ump says he calls them as he sees them. The third says they ain't nothing until he calls them.

This bothers most of us. Athletes' prowess should be judged on the basis of their abilities, not their nationalities. Skill should be the measure, nothing else. Sporting competitions are meant to be strict meritocracies, pure examples of the most qualified rising to the top; contests should be objective and fair. In reality, there are other considerations besides skill. Athletes get injured and competitions aren't rescheduled, so the winners are not always the best, but the lucky. And the phenomenon of the "home court advantage" indicates that something other than skill enters into the equation.

We would like it to be otherwise. Merit should be based on ability, not status or breed. On the other hand, traditional societies have a different hierarchy of values. Royalty is royalty not because a person makes a good queen but because she is next in line to rule. Nepotism is standard in tight-knit groups; the more intense the loyalty, the greater the tendency to favor our own kind. This is rooted in the sense that those closest to us deserve favored treatment. The circle widens from family to kin to clan to tribe to nation, the ripples of the circle becoming increasingly weak.

Martin Luther King Jr. called for a reversal of the traditional thinking when he said that we should judge people on the basis of their character, not the color of their skin. Let each person prove herself without the impediments of biased loyalty. So, in our example, the right thing for Sally to do is to ignore race and give the job to the best-qualified person. She should close her eyes, ignore a person's background, and let competency speak for itself. This is what a democracy is all about—it is the American Dream.

No one should suffer because of his race. Fairness requires color blindness.

## Taking Specific Needs into Account

What, if anything, can be said on Sally's behalf? Is there any moral justification for Sally's hiring Tisha, someone less qualified than others applying to do the same work? We don't know what Sally has in mind when she hires Tisha. Maybe Sally dislikes nonblacks. If that is the case, then the decision is based on prejudice, which hardly qualifies as a moral claim. But let's assume that isn't her reason, that her decision rests on something more noble instead.

Rather than using equality as her yardstick, Sally chooses equity. Equality treats everyone the same regardless of his condition; equity tries to even things out. Equality assumes that everyone starts from the same place; equity assumes that people start from different positions. Equality assumes that society is already fair; equity assumes that society needs to be made fair. Equality looks at the present moment; equity takes the past into consideration and makes predictions about the future.

Ethical judgments depend in part on how we understand and interpret the facts of the situation. So part of whether you accept Sally's reasoning depends upon how you analyze American society. If you believe that racism is an insignificant factor, then Sally is wrong. If you believe that privileges accrue to whites because of their race, then Sally's decision makes moral sense. It seems beyond dispute that the economic gap between blacks and whites in America is closing. At the same time, blacks still lag far behind whites in most social and economic indicators. Whites see the first statement as most significant; blacks tend to focus on the second part. This, in turn, leads to differing evaluations of the morality of preferential treatment given to blacks.

## History and Sociology as Factors in Making Ethical Choices

Many whites who oppose affirmative action fear that it leads to less-qualified blacks being hired and promoted over more-qualified whites, while many blacks are afraid that without affirmative action, less-qualified whites will be hired or promoted over more-qualified blacks. Differently lived realities mean different interpretations of the facts of life. Regarding racial relations, this has led to, in the words of journalist David K. Shipler, "a country of strangers." Whites tend to believe that racism is a thing of the past and has no bearing on the world today. African Americans tend to believe that they are disadvantaged in many subtle ways, all adding up to something less than a fair shake. Whites, therefore, see affirmative action as reverse discrimination while blacks see it as helping to bring things up to where they should be.

Sally may give Tisha the job because she is afraid of a lawsuit. This and other self-serving reasons count not as moral but as prudential. But assuming that Sally's interpretation of social reality is close to the truth and her intention is to do her part to make up for a larger injustice experienced by African Americans, there are still other factors to take into account before deciding whether her action is morally correct. It is one thing if it is her own business. Then her decision would be cleaner. If she wants to pay for Tisha's inefficiency herself by making less profit, she can do that. She is free to do what she wants with her own business, even take it bankrupt.

But if Sally is working for someone else, she has a larger web of people to whom she is accountable, primarily her boss or the stockholders, or in the case of a nonprofit organization, the members or taxpayers. She can't decide on her own to rectify a social wrong and make someone else pay for it. In a sense, what she is doing is not so different from writing a check from the company's accounts to her favorite charity. This means that when Sally decides to hire Tisha, she must also take on the task of making Tisha a more efficient worker and do this is such a way that the cost is truly hers, not the company's. Sally may have to train Tisha, work more closely with her than she would with other secretaries, give her encouragement, all without doing less elsewhere. Maybe she could even pay for Tisha to attend secretarial school, at night or on the weekends.

## The Value of Diversity

Having said all this, there is yet another dimension to this vignette. Sally may not be thinking in large social terms. She may not care about racial prejudice. She may not even think that Tisha deserves a boost or should somehow be compensated for past wrong. Instead, she may think that the best secretary, in the long run, may not be the person who performs best during an interview or starts out with the best measurable skills, such as typing and taking dictation. Sally could be looking at the situation in purely business terms.

Tisha, in Sally's view, may possess other, intangible qualities that are real assets to the company. Sally may take the position as that of several universities do, that there is a value in diversity itself. There is something enriching about being with those who are different. Perhaps Sally thinks that Tisha would bring a new creativity to the business, a needed leavening in an otherwise flat setting. In this case, Sally would be investing in the future. She should work with Tisha to get her up to speed so that Tisha would then contribute to the business in a way that white candidates simply could not.

There is nothing wrong with businesses putting off short-term gains for long-term investments. It isn't reverse discrimination, but more like a prudent business decision. One can argue about whether racial diversity really has such a value, but this is different from saying that it is unfair to whites.

Sally's willingness to extend herself to Tisha may not lower the company's efficiency, but rather may well contribute to it. Other factors may contribute to Tisha's success at work—Sally's help being one of them. While objectively Tisha may not be the best person for the job when she is hired, I hope that Sally believes that Tisha can become as good as any other person for the job, if given the right support. Sally is taking a chance on her potential. I also hope that Sally isn't doing this without the support of her superiors, if she isn't the owner herself. Without a commitment to affirmative action from the top, Tisha is likely to fail. As hard as it is to create a diversified workplace, it is just as difficult to maintain it. Tisha's failure on the job likely would lead to reinforcing stereotypes on both sides of the racial divide: you see, I told you blacks aren't really competent; I told you so, whites are happy to see African Americans fail.

If Sally can't find support for diversifying her workplace, if her superiors find no value in such an arrangement, if the only value that the company endorses is increasing profits (or however a nonprofit organization measures success), then Sally has to decide for herself how important her ethical values are. If she can't square her own conscience with her work, she may have to quit. If she doesn't quit, she may have to examine her own conscience. There is an adage that everyone has a price. I don't know if this is true. But it is true that those committed to moral behavior sometimes have to pay a price for their scruples.

# 21

❦

# Is It Moral for Me to Take Advantage of a Technicality?

Catherine receives a ticket for parking in a loading zone on a Sunday afternoon. She has parked there several times before and has never seen trucks loading or anyone receiving a ticket. When she examines her ticket, she discovers that the wrong license plate number has been entered. There would be no way to trace the ticket if she doesn't pay it. She mails the ticket back with the payment the next day.

Some questions to ask yourself:

1. Should you be held responsible for making a mistake?
2. Can something be wrong if you acted for the right reason?
3. Is there a difference between the spirit of the law and the letter of the law?
4. Is something wrong even if you won't be found out?
5. Is Catherine acting ethically?

# The Problem:
# Doing Right Because It's Right
# versus Doing Right Because of
# the Fear of Getting Caught

Catherine found herself in the position of the shepherd Gyges in ancient Greece. One day while in the field, he found a ring that had the magical property of making him invisible whenever he twisted it. As soon as he was aware of this power, Gyges went to the king to provide the monthly report on behalf of all the shepherds. When he reached the court, he turned the ring, became invisible, and immediately seduced the queen, slew the king, and took the throne.

Glaucon, who told this story to Socrates, used it to illustrate that the only reason people act morally is that they fear punishment. Take away the fear, and everyone will only be interested in himself and therefore will be immoral.

"For all men believe in their hearts that injustice is far more profitable to the individual than justice, and he who argues as I have been supposing, will say that they are right," Glaucon concluded.

This story claims that people will act morally so they won't be punished. Actually, some research by psychologists has examined this very question. As you can imagine, the picture is mixed. Some people are, in fact, motivated by the fear of punishment. This is a low level of moral development and it fits the developmental stage of young children. Moral motivation gets more complicated as people get older, although some people remain at the earlier stage of motivation. There are many, though, whose motive for acting morally has to do with compassion, loyalty, and a sense of justice.

The other consideration raised by the Gyges story is this:

Assuming that you won't get caught, should you do the right thing anyway? This addresses the question of what you ought to do, which is the real philosophical matter.

## The Letter of the Law
## as It Applies to the Lawmakers

There's no question about what Catherine should do, right? Amitai Etzioni, a professor at George Washington University and leading social philosopher, doesn't think so. When I asked him about Catherine's problem, he said, "What's the question? If I do something which I do not know is wrong, and nobody told me, and there is no reasonable way of finding out, what is the issue?"

Not so fast. Even seemingly obvious and trivial problems aren't always simple. Catherine's situation on closer scrutiny reveals complex ethical considerations.

We often read in the papers or see on TV that a seemingly guilty person is let off because of a technicality. A thief confesses to his crime but is released because he wasn't read his Miranda rights. Or a murderer isn't convicted, even though the gun with his fingerprints was found, because the police obtained the weapon without a proper search warrant.

This makes sense from one point of view. There is a good reason for the accused—even those whose guilt isn't in question— to be let off on technicalities, even for serious crimes. If this weren't so, the government could easily run roughshod over the rights of the individual. The theory is that unless authorities meticulously follow the law, no one is safe from abuses of power. Without close attention to proper procedures, the police could easily become thugs, the government a dictatorship. So while someone may have committed an offense, unless the police carry out their duties scrupulously as required by law, the person is not legally guilty. The criminal justice system is required to follow the law itself, and when it doesn't, having its case thrown out against the accused, in effect, punishes it.

# The Letter of the Law as It Applies to an Individual

Catherine's offense isn't as serious as that of a criminal's. It is a petty civil violation. In addition, she isn't trying to get away with anything. Just the opposite. She didn't mean to violate the no-parking regulation. She really thought that the sign didn't apply to Sundays and that she could park her car there. Once I parked at a meter at 8 A.M. and didn't put in my quarter. When I went to get my car a half hour later, I had a ticket. I went to traffic court and pleaded innocent. I explained to the judge that I knew of nowhere else on Long Island where meters required money before 9 A.M. The judge said I should have read the sign. I argued that no reasonable person would have bothered to read the sign, since there was no reason to think that one street in one village would be an exception to the rule. The judge appeared to enjoy my jailhouse-lawyer defense, then dismissed my case.

Catherine, like me, broke the law. However, she wouldn't even have to argue her case by pointing to extenuating circumstances. Technically, the law was on her side because her parking ticket was written incorrectly. When New York City issued its first jaywalking summons in 1998 to a woman who breached a barrier at a crosswalk, she didn't have to pay the fine because the officer cited the wrong statute on her ticket. Furthermore, in Catherine's case, no one need even know that she even received a ticket. She could throw it away and the police would never be the wiser.

But Catherine isn't concerned about the legal niceties; she

did what she thought was the right thing from an ethical point of view. She broke the law, she was caught, and she should pay the penalty even though she could get away with it.

Perhaps she was foolish, for she couldn't be traced. Besides, fines aren't meant as revenue enhancement, but are a method used by government to exact pain on the guilty so they will think twice about committing the offense again.

Hasn't Catherine learned her lesson even if she doesn't pay the fine? Perhaps so. The next time she receives a fine, it isn't likely that the ticket will be written incorrectly. Therefore, whether she pays the fine makes no difference regarding her future behavior. Either she cares about getting caught or it makes no difference to her. If she believes that the law is wrong to begin with, or she is so wealthy that paying a fine of whatever amount makes no material difference, then she might choose to park there whenever it is convenient. But if she accepts the necessity for such parking regulations and paying fines bothers her, then she will choose to obey the sign the next time.

So if it doesn't make a difference whether she pays the fine this time, perhaps she is being overly scrupulous. Catherine's reason seems to be simple and straightforward: she knowingly broke the law and deserves the punishment. That she can get away with it is beside the point. She took a chance and lost. She knew that was a possibility when she parked there.

## Moral Reasons to Get Away with It

I can see only two moral considerations for Catherine not paying the fine: one, she is destitute; or two, the law is unfair. Catherine would not starve if she paid the fine, so the first reason doesn't apply. The second might, however. The sign reasonably applies to workdays, not Sundays. The regulation makes little or no sense for the day when Catherine parked there. A person could fairly believe that the sign was not meant to apply to Sundays.

She still might have grounds on which not to pay if she were to challenge the regulation as being unreasonable. Rather than ignore the ticket, she might make public her opposition to the regulation. This would mean informing the parking bureau that she received a parking ticket but refuses to pay it. Catherine might lose her driver's license, have her salary garnisheed, and otherwise receive rough treatment. It is doubtful she would succeed against the crunching bureaucracy. But this does seem to be the only legitimate route to follow, however futile, for someone who wishes to challenge a law perceived as unfair within a democratic society.

The assumption here is that despite its obvious limitations and unfulfilled promises, the government ultimately reflects the will of the populace. If laws and regulations were truly capricious and subject to the whims of the powerful, then no one would have a moral obligation to follow them. But if the process allows for change through peaceful means, then we either obey the law, try to change it, or openly challenge it, accepting the likely punishment.

Socrates made this argument in explaining why he rejected the opportunity to escape after receiving the death penalty. Of course, Catherine isn't charged with subversive teaching and she isn't going to be executed. But the logic of the argument is the same. What distinguishes her situation is the pettiness of the offense.

## Rationalizing and Justifying

Catherine refuses to resort to either of the two most common reasons—rationalizations, really—for not paying the fine: one, she can get away with it; and two, everybody is doing it. The first reason admits wrongdoing but assumes guilt only if she is caught, while the second excuses the guilt by making it unexceptional. Neither reason is a justification, only an explanation. And an explanation by itself is not an excuse.

Having said this, I believe that she didn't think she was doing anything wrong in the first instance. A reasonable person could have assumed that that sign didn't reflect the reality of the situation, and therefore Catherine has no moral obligation to pay the fine. There are ancient laws on the books that make it a crime to do the silliest thing. If a police officer gave you a ticket because you broke one of the laws that you didn't know about and no one cared about and was otherwise never enforced, you wouldn't be morally obligated to pay the fine.

While ignorance may be no excuse as far as the law is concerned, it is a factor that militates against moral obligations. Generally speaking, we are immoral when we act out of badwill or contrary to a generally accepted standard of just or compassionate behavior. None of this applies to Catherine, so she wouldn't be immoral to tear up the ticket and toss it into the nearest garbage can.

## A Moral Reason to Pay the Fine

Nevertheless, Catherine isn't wrong in paying the fine. The cop who filled out the ticket should have been as conscientious about his job as Catherine is about doing the right thing. But in paying the fine, Catherine is living consistently with an internalized sense of right and wrong. As a matter of conscience, she has to pay the fine. For her it is integrity, not fear, that leads her to pay it.

Although Catherine could get away with not paying the fine, she can't get away from herself. Her moral sense and her sense of herself are bound together. This is a desirable quality, provided that she does not become weighed down by petty offenses and can distinguish between the truly significant moral issues of life and the minor ones.

Earnest consistency, one that sees in every cranny moral threats, can also be dulling, making one into a moral cop, a bore whom others want to avoid. At the same time, to care about ethical behavior, even if others think you odd, is a sign of maturity.

❦

# 22

# Should My Personal Values
# Stay at Home?

Lyn is a job developer with a refugee assistance program. While many of the refugees are well educated, their English-speaking ability is limited. Most of the placements are in menial labor. A manufacturer of military hardware notifies her office about openings. The company pays well and will provide English classes in order to promote the new workers to positions commensurate with their real abilities.

In her personal life as a political activist, Lyn opposes military expenditures. However, she decides to send the refugees to the job interview.

Some questions to ask yourself:

1. How do you decide what your conscience demands?
2. How do you balance personal values with the values and objectives of those you work for?
3. Should your personal values be set aside in the workplace?
4. Is consistency between personal values and marketplace values possible or even desirable?
5. Is Lyn doing the right thing?

# The Problem:
# Personal Values versus
# Professional Standards

Life would be simple if all our values harmonized with one another and were consistent with the values of the community around us. This is the objective of Confucian ethics, where harmony is viewed as a prerequisite for happiness. Over the centuries, this desire to eliminate disharmony led to a rigid system of rule-following that reinforced social inequities between men and women and rulers and followers.

As we have learned from stories about gangsters, there is often honor among thieves. They are square with one another, and many are loving and compassionate toward those who are close to them. But they apply a different set of values when they go about their business. Ethics is set aside, and right makes might.

The same disconnect between living by one set of values in our homes and another at work is a common problem. We want to do the right thing, but what is the right thing when different situations seem to require different responses?

# Conscience in the Workplace

This anecdote is a true one, involving my wife, Lyn, who worked for the Adelphi University Refugee Assistance Program as a job placement officer. At that time, much of Long Island's economy was based on military-related companies involved with aircraft manufacturing. The best-paying jobs with the greatest possibility for advancement were mainly in that industry. There was no question that it was better to work for Grumman than for McDonald's, if the measure of a good job was calculated in pay and working conditions. So she often felt pulled between wanting to find the best jobs for her clients and not wanting to support the weapons industry.

Lyn faced what many socially conscious and conscientious workers confront—a conflict between personal convictions and the demands of the workplace. On the one hand, Lyn wanted to do her job conscientiously, believing that finding good jobs for people was a good thing. On the other hand, she took her political values seriously. For her, this meant opposing the "military-industrial complex," as defined by Dwight Eisenhower in his farewell speech as president of the country.

What we need to do may not be in harmony with what we want the world to be like. Lyn's dilemma points out that even those in the not-for-profit sector can have this problem.

## Some Ways to Avoid the Problem

One way out of the conflict is to redefine the conditions so that there is no dilemma. If, for example, you believe that capitalism is in itself an ethical system that works to everyone's advantage all the time, then everyone's good is served by putting aside personal values and simply doing your job. Financier George Soros summed up this approach by writing, "Laissez-faire capitalism holds that the common good is best served by the uninhibited pursuit of self-interest." In other words, let the refugees pursue their own interests—with Lyn's help—and everything will work out for the moral best. In this case, though, the question remains, what is Lyn's best ethical interest?

Another way to attain consistency in values is to avoid the problem in the first place by taking a detached stance. Some religions promote such a position, regarding this world as somehow a pale reflection of a more real other world. Some artists have tried this approach as well. Matthew Arnold, for example, thought that the true poet "will not maintain a hostile attitude towards the false pretensions of his age; he will content himself with not being overwhelmed by them. He will esteem himself fortunate if he can succeed in banishing from his mind all feelings of contradiction, and irritation, and impatience."

But I don't know a poet today who doesn't experience the contradiction between a dedication toward art and the commercial demands of the publishing industry, which increasingly displaces an interest in literary values with a concern for profit margins. Imagination, freedom, and money are the three legs of the artist's stool, and they are always in a wobbly relationship to one another.

I also know how difficult it is to get agreement among members of one family, except those run by autocrats. Not only are there differences of taste, but there are also varying interests. What children need and want is not the same as for adults, what a husband or wife needs isn't always the same thing, not everyone agrees upon what is owed to grown brothers and sisters, and so on. Public lives are no different in this regard, only more complex. We are not dealing with three or four or five people but with 250 million, if we confine our thinking to present national borders. From this I conclude that politics will always be with us, that it is incumbent upon us to live a public life for the interests of all people to be fairly represented, and that the outcome of our efforts will always be less than what we want.

I don't see how it is possible to live a life in which our deepest ethical principles aren't challenged at least some of the time. Still, to what extent should Lyn's political concerns intrude upon her work? I presented this problem to Father Bill Brisotti, pacifist and social justice activist who has spent time in Central America working with peasant farmers. Brisotti is a parish priest whose ministry is with the Hispanic community. I asked him in particular because his commitment to social justice is without equal.

Indeed, he has been arrested several times for acts of civil disobedience. I think his response is so thoughtful that I want to repeat all that he said.

# Living Consistently

Brisotti writes:

> If Lyn's opposition to military expenditures were based on true, moral convictions, she would not send the refugees to the job interview. She has acquiesced to shallow expediency, thereby inviting the refugees to join her as part of the problem, rather than as part of the solution. It's like inviting a death row inmate to work on keeping the electric chair in good repair, paying him well, giving him nice privileges, and, eventually, frying him in his polished and diligently maintained death machine.
>
> The military manufacturer pays well and offers enticing benefits and opportunities due to the wastefully misguided spending priorities of the United States government. Seemingly unlimited funds are afforded to military matters, further limiting public monies available for the infrastructure providing education, health care, transportation, and other necessities for ordinary people, especially the poor. Cost overruns are no problem for the "black hole" of military expenditures.
>
> However, Lyn's decision should not be founded on an unnuanced equanimity of values of what might be bought with public funds—perhaps a little less to buy machines to kill peasants attempting to improve their lot in third world countries, making a little more available to educate some of their survivors in Chicago. People attempting to "assist" refugees have to be aware of, and to take into account, the larger picture of their lives, and what is truly beneficial to them.
>
> The refugees come to Lyn for guidance in their plight. In most cases, they were forced to leave their families, homelands, and all that is dear to them, due to military repression and severe economic hardship. Even if they are, as our vignette suggests, part of the relatively well-educated minority, the "men with guns" have made a decent life

impossible, skewing the balance of power interminably in favor of the ruling elite.

The socioeconomic dysfunction of a refugee working for a military manufacturer is rather clear. The worldwide trade of military technology and hardware expands the base of grinding poverty, foments international as well as intranational hostilities, bolsters the control of the dominant elite, and produces refugees. The refugee would be laboring to earn money to survive here in an environment hostile toward poor immigrants, while sending money to family members at home, struggling against forces within his or her homeland propped up by the ready availability of the very weapons he or she is working to build. This is the classic "Catch-22," where his diligent efforts to resolve his problems are aggravating them.

# Trying Harder

A true advocate for refugees would have no trouble finding uncompromised resources whose sole purpose is to help the refugees be proficient in the English language. I find this similar to the United States Army, Navy, Air Force, or Marines propagandizing inner-city youth with promises of college education, career training, and other avenues of upward mobility, or at least, an escape from the ghetto. Find a frustrated, hungry person and offer him free food as well as light at the distant end of the tunnel; unfortunately, the food is laced with cyanide and the light at the end of the tunnel is a fast-moving, oncoming train. He'll devour his food and run toward the light, if he's desperate enough.

From a moral perspective, Lyn's action is difficult to defend. Perhaps she thoroughly explained the situation to the refugees beforehand, and let them make the decision. However, our vignette indicates she decided to send the refugees to the job interview, which seems to connote a certain moral persuasiveness on her part as an authoritarian figure. She certainly must bear some responsibility for the moral implications of the work of any of these people, if indeed, they go to work for that company.

Lyn is helping propagate the lie that death-dealing industries, with smooth promotional techniques and bottomless resources, are simply a legitimate part of the occupational landscape. You can sell automobiles or Trident submarines, both are A-OK. Some may even argue that more people die because of automobiles than nuclear subs. This is probably true, superficially speaking, considering direct deaths through accidents as well as indirect deaths through cancer or other illness with auto emission pollution as a contributing factor. However, after further study, you see that the very existence of a Trident sub has already caused death through its theft of resources, through radiation-induced illness at all stages of the nuclear fuel cycle, through its major role in the U.S. arsenal and that of the rest of the members of the Nuclear Club, maintaining military dominance and controlling the destinies of third world nations, holding the nuclear gun at the head of every living man, woman, and child on the face of the earth. How else could less than 6 percent of the world's population—those in the U.S.A.,—control most of the world's resources, feeding our insatiable gluttony, while thousands of children die daily from hunger?

Lyn's protégé would probably find success in the industry that makes the U.S.A. the world's leading merchant of weapons, particularly to third world countries. Her agency may even get funding from General Electric, Westinghouse, or some other major weapons producer happy to be in partnership with her.

Lyn did not do the right thing.

I agree with much of Brisotti's commentary, but I disagree with his conclusion. First, here's where I agree with him. If Lyn didn't care about public life or if she believed that there was no connection between private and public selves, she wouldn't have a problem. But she makes no such distinction, so her personal commitments collide with her obligation to carry on with her chosen work. She isn't alone in this. Many people find a gap between their personal beliefs and professional requirements.

Sheriff John McDougall in Florida is a good example of this. A Franciscan seminarian for seven years, as a Catholic, he is staunchly opposed to abortion. He wrote a letter to the head of an abortion clinic that he would carry out his duty to protect "even a baby killer like yourself" but would also assist the protesters "who wish to protect the misguided mothers who come to your clinic of death." He is quoted in the *New York Times* as saying, "I'm in the business of protecting people and it's frustrating that I can't protect these little babies. You have to speak out on social ills."

In the vignette, Lyn is caught in a similar bind. She, too, must choose, this time between her own antimilitary convictions and the welfare of those who use the services of her agency. I presume that Lyn wouldn't work for a military contractor herself. She would probably find an alternative and, I suspect, she would take a job for less pay than to be associated with the military. Being employed by such a company is tantamount to abetting a cause that she opposes. But here she is not making a choice about her own career, but about the future of others.

## Conflicting Values Are Part of Life

Now, here's where Brisotti and I disagree. Lyn doesn't have an obligation to offer the refugees any and all jobs that she learns about. There probably is a market for hired assassins, but she wouldn't place someone in that job, because the work itself is criminal. Similarly, she has no obligation to place someone in a criminal setting, such as a sweatshop. Those limits are pretty clear, and enforcing them doesn't rely upon her personal evaluation.

There are other areas that are not so clear. Say she knows of a good job in which the employee will be paid off the books. The work itself isn't illegitimate but the method of payment is since, at the very least, it circumvents paying taxes. Does her obligation extend to recommending employment about which she has questions but that the employer and employee both find acceptable—

is the morality of the particular job only a matter of conscience between the two parties?

In the particular instance facing Lyn, the work isn't illegal and the means of employment are aboveboard and legitimate. In fact, if it were possible to leave aside the product involved, it is an excellent job. Lyn, however, cannot consider the type of industry irrelevant. But she is not willing to impose that viewpoint on others. If the refugee opposes the military also, then the refugee will turn down the job.

I think that Lyn is willing to make this compromise because she isn't fully committed to eliminating the military, doesn't find the industry repulsive enough or its work so horrendous that she cannot assist it even this much. For example, if the state were looking for an executioner to work the electric chair and she was opposed to capital punishment, it is unlikely that she would offer the position as a good job opportunity. It probably would so disgust her that she would quit rather than aid state-sanctioned killing.

## Compromising One Value for the Sake of Another

Although she also opposes state-sanctioned killing known as war, the extent of her conviction is not as thorough. It is more like the vegetarian who won't eat meat but will tolerate eggs, drink milk, and wear leather shoes. This is not to dispute the significance of such principles, only that the principles are not total. They are guided by additional considerations. Lyn may oppose war in general but not all wars, whereas her opposition to the death penalty may be unconditional.

In this vignette, there is another important consideration aside from her opposition to the military. Lyn has a commitment to the individuals who depend upon her as a source of decent employment. The agency she works for doesn't tell refugees that it will offer them only politically acceptable positions. The agency doesn't make such judgments and neither does Lyn, not because she thinks such considerations are unimportant but because she believes that people are free to make their own political decisions, including what kind of jobs they will work at. Respect for the conscience of each person and a tolerance for political differences are reflected in this neutral stance.

Whether you judge Lyn's decision as correct depends in part on whether you yourself oppose the military. If war and its accouterments are assessed as evil, then any relationship to it is also evil. But it is possible to object to a policy and work to overturn it without at the same time rejecting everyone who has contact with the implementation of that policy. The compromises we make between private and public lives are a matter of finding a balance so that we aren't fanatical or indifferent.

The mistake I think Lyn could make would be to withhold the information from her clients. If she so strongly objects to the nature of the job placement, she should resign as a matter of conscience. (Similarly, if Sheriff McDougall cannot protect the abortion clinic workers, he should quit as a law officer.) But as long as Lyn stays, her work demands that she find the best-paying jobs under the best working conditions with the greatest possibility of promotion. The only consideration is whether the job is legal. That is what the clients think she is there for, and they are right. Lyn can try to persuade them to take whatever political action she thinks desirable, but that she must do as a private citizen.

# 23

*❧*

# What Should I Do
# with Money I Find?

Irma makes a telephone call from a pay phone booth. When she hangs up, a rush of quarters spews out. She put the money in her purse and walks away, never returning the money to the telephone company.

Some questions to ask yourself:

1. Does it matter who lost the money?
2. Does it matter how much is found?
3. Does it matter how needy she is?
4. Does it matter whether or not you are likely to be found out?
5. Does it matter what she intends to do with the money?
6. Is Irma doing the right thing?

## The Problem: Something Earned
## versus a Stroke of Good Luck

Money and morality are often an uncomfortable fit, especially if the money falls into one's lap, so to speak. Who doesn't want more money? As a child I heard that possession is nine-tenths of the law. So even the law seems to side with the finder, and tough luck for the loser.

Not long ago a New York City cabdriver found $10,000 in the backseat of his cab and returned it to its rightful owner. A group of parochial school children happened to be visiting City Hall the day Mayor Giuliani was honoring this upright citizen. Hoping to use the occasion as a lesson in moral rectitude, the mayor asked the students what they would do if they found such a sum of money. He was sure the students would answer in the morally acceptable way. There was no choice, right? The students didn't think so either. For them it was a no-brainer.

They answered quickly and in unison, "Keep it!"

I have gotten much the same response whenever I've related the anecdote about Irma. Hardly anyone has said that he would return the money. One reason is practical: "What should I do, put the quarters back in the telephone?" Or, "Do you expect me to send a check to the phone company?" Some think along the lines of, "Even if I sent it, they wouldn't know what to do with it, they're so fouled up."

The story does raise another kind of moral question, though, revealed by those who don't give practical reasons for keeping the money but something quite different. They say one of two things—either "It's payback time. I'm ripped off all the time. It's only a matter of getting even," or "It's a giant corporation. They'll never miss it."

# The Difference between What People Will Do and What People Ought to Do

Irma's story is a nice illustration of the difference between descriptive ethics—what people actually do—and prescriptive ethics—

what someone ought to do. This is the difference between, say, knowing that nearly everyone lies at one time or another and saying that lying is wrong. Descriptive ethics is a sociological or psychological proposition. It focuses upon what people really do, and it may ask why there might be a gap between what they say they should do and what they actually do.

Prescriptive ethics looks at morality from the point of view of establishing what someone ought to do. It leaves aside motivational considerations and concerns itself exclusively with what is ethically correct.

The difference between descriptive and prescriptive ethics can be explained by way of analogy. You go to the doctor because you're not feeling well. Your doctor examines you. She looks down your throat, takes some X rays, and asks for a family history. When she's done, she tells you what's wrong with you, "Well, you've got monoglucososyitus."

"Gee, Doc," you say, "I guess that's not so good."

"You'll be okay," she says. "Here, have the druggist fill this. Take two pills three times a day and you'll be fine."

That's the prescription the doctor gives you. It's a type of advice. You are free to either accept this advice or reject it. The doctor can't force you to fill the prescription or to follow the regimen that she laid out for you. But let's say you've decided to have the prescription filled. You now go home and take your pills, three times a day after meals. If you are like many patients, when you start to feel better you stop taking your medication.

It's sometimes like this in morals: you analyze the situation, know what you should do, and then, like many people in a similar situation, don't do it at all or don't do it thoroughly.

I wondered what a business owner would think of Irma's actions. I asked Laura Bernstein, who is a third-generation owner of a medium-sized children's sleepwear manufacturing company.

"Much as I'd like to think otherwise, and it's certainly not something I care to admit in print, I'm forced to confront the fact: I would keep the change," she says.

It seems like winning on a slot machine. It's like one of those freaks of nature, a chance occurrence. It's sort of divine retribution, a low-level revenge against the impersonal machinery of modern, bureaucratic society.

Bernstein says, "Taking the telephone change would be so instinctive a response that we do so virtually unaware of our behavior. Wouldn't you take the money? I ask that not to justify my action but to point out that the issue, I believe, is that so few of us actually see Irma—or ourselves—as doing anything wrong."

Clearly, the money isn't Irma's. She didn't earn it or win it in a game of chance. It isn't even like finding money on the street. Here Irma knows the source of the money. It came from the pay phone. She knows who owns the phone: the label on it tells her it belongs to Verizon. Irma's getting the money is like finding a wallet with the owner's name in it.

Is it right to keep something that isn't yours, when it is someone else's and you know who that someone is? The honorable person returns something he sees falling out of an individual's pocket. It is only a small step to theft from picking it up himself without making an attempt to return it. Similarly, it is right that an attempt be made to locate the owner of a lost object.

## Three Reasons for Keeping the Money

Then what justification, if any, is there in keeping the coins from the phone? Three serious reasons can be given: one, the impracticality of returning a small sum; two, that phone company profits are too high and this is an opportunity to even the score (A variation of number two is that the company has cheated you in the past, so this helps balance the account.); and three, moral responsibilities are owed to individuals, not corporations.

## Being Practical

The first reason isn't a moral one but a practical one. Is it or isn't it impractical to return money to the phone company? In a clever experiment, Laura Bernstein's friend Anastasia called the phone company and pretended to be Irma. The operator at the Verizon billing office was quite baffled by the question and put Anastasia on hold for several minutes. "We have no department to deal with this," she finally declared. "You should just keep the money."

But the operator wasn't speaking for the company, only herself. Irma could mail them the money. Will it make any difference to a multibillion-dollar corporation if it gets a few dollars from Irma? No. But judging the rightness of behavior cannot rest upon whether our efforts make a difference, although if our efforts count for very little then the severity of the judgment may vary. (It is a generally accepted idea among ethical philosophers that principles exist only if it is possible for the action to actually be fulfilled. An *ought* entails an *able*. So if I can do much and don't, the moral judgment is more severe than if I can do very little and don't.)

In this anecdote the amount is so small that it makes very little difference to the company's balance sheet; it is also so small that it makes virtually no difference in Irma's life now that she has it. But it isn't the amount of money that matters or whether the phone company will miss the money. The moral point hinges on something else, which I will explain in a moment.

## Getting Even

The second argument made for keeping the money is the one of retribution, balancing the scales—I was cheated in the past, so the bonanza is really deserved. Keeping the windfall is getting even. Many people I know have contempt for large corporations, even though they may have never suffered directly from them. I understand this. By their very nature, they are easy to detest—their scale, impersonality, and wealth beyond comprehension. A company that makes billions in profits while firing workers to reduce the workforce leaves something ethically to be desired.

A society in which a few gain incredible wealth because of corporate investments and profits while others are shoved onto unemployment lines or suffer from reduced living standards also is less than morally exemplary. Some who use the reason of retribution continue their argument something like this: since there is no way to overturn the monstrosity, keeping the money is justifiable. It is a credit on the side of the ledger for the little guy. If you believe that it is right to return something to someone who has lost it, such as money fallen out of a pocket, you do so only if you believe that the person who lost it had a right to it in the first place. You wouldn't return stolen goods to a thief. So it's okay to keep the money because the phone company has stolen from customers in the past.

Bernstein responds this way: "What's had tremendous impact to shape my thinking about an ethical dilemma like this one is that I have been working in a business setting for many years, and especially because I own part of a small business—we manufacture children's clothes. Perhaps I see things differently now, because if my family and I owned the malfunctioning phone, it would be our money that was being stolen. So big business isn't somebody else, it's me."

The argument for taking money from big business is one of resentment, not reason. Few people I've met who make such an argument have really thought through what an alternative to corporate capitalism might be like, in particular as it relates to a utility such as the phone company. Or if they have, they haven't done much to bring about a politically altered state. If the phone company were a thief, then its chairman ought to be in jail. But to keep the money as though this were the crusade of a modern Robin Hood is romantic hoodwinking, a playacting that is a poor justification for keeping something that isn't one's own.

To keep the money on these grounds shows a misguided political consciousness, thinking that keeping the coins will bring down the phone company. Maybe the phone company ought to be made a public corporation, maybe executives ought not to be allowed to make huge amounts of money. These are important policy issues that ought to be discussed and confronted in a serious manner. But keeping the money isn't real political action. It is a rationalization for keeping something that doesn't belong to you. It may well be that, contrary to the belief that keeping the money is somehow helping to change society for the better, it may actually do the opposite. You may think you have discharged your responsibility to take real action. Losing a few dollars in loose change doesn't harm the phone company. Therefore, Irma's keeping the money has no practical consequence in political terms. The only practical thing about her behavior is that she has a few more dollars in her own pocket.

Banks are equally a piece of corporate society. Yet many people, if given the wrong amount of money by a teller at a bank, will return the overpayment. Why? Because they know that at the end of the day the teller is accountable for the missing money. She can be fired for incompetence. Because the possible consequences are known, namely the firing of a particular individual with whom one has had personal contact, the morally sensitive person doesn't hesitate in returning the money to the bank. But, say the extra money were given at an ATM, where the error is electronic and not personal, then the question resembles the one in this vignette. No person will suffer from this mistake, one might think. Therefore it is mere foolishness to be so honest as to return the money if unasked.

We make many ethical decisions based upon the ability to see and understand the outcome of our actions. Hurting people is wrong, so we try to avoid doing that. Bernstein makes much the same point when she asks, "Don't teenagers find it easier to shoplift at Kmart than at the local candy store where their schoolmate's mom in working part-time? The problem is that we suffer from the lack of community and connection in our lives that makes so much of what we experience *anonymous*. In an urban high-rise apartment, where we know so few of our neighbors, who can tell whether the wallet we find in the elevator belongs to the elderly antiques dealer across the hall or someone we'll never know?"

## Obligations Apply to People, Not Institutions

The third argument is that ethics is a matter between people. Since the phone company isn't a person, we don't have moral obligations in relation to it. The phone company isn't an individual, despite the legal fiction created by the courts. Therefore, we can't see the harm that comes from keeping the money. Bernstein comments with these examples: "If a dry cleaner forgets to bill me for my cardigan sweater set with the extra pearl buttons, if the florist sends over a bouquet and bills me for plain carnations instead of the yellow sweetheart roses I actually received, do I correct them? Is it my moral obligation to do so? What about the waiter who forgets the chocolate cake I've ordered when he tallies the check? But if that waiter were a college friend or a distant cousin, would I point out the mistake in the check? Maybe it's easier to cheat in business: we can hide behind our suits and ties and desk accessories. Business is a game, after all: we assemble a team on the field, strategize for touchdown tactics, talk of winners and losers. It's a battle to beat out our competition to the playoffs. And if there are a few shady moves on the way to picking up the trophy, isn't that all part of the game? My 'nice guy' doesn't get to the Super Bowl."

## The Reason to Return the Money: Little Things Lead to Big Ones

In sports there is an expression "No harm, no foul." The same could apply here. The amount in our story is so small, the circumstances so unusual, and the source such a deep pocket that in essence no one is hurt. Without an injured party, there is no moral transgression.

The harm, it seems to me, comes from the blot left upon ourselves by feeling entitled to keep something that doesn't belong to us. It is a form of dishonesty. The question is to what extent this makes it easier for us to justify similar but more significant matters in the future. Is it the beginning of what philosophers call the slippery slope leading to frequent rationalizations? Is it the beginning of self-deception?

I can see only one reason to keep the money—it adds a little spice to life. Perhaps it is excessively scrupulous to return the money, and one shouldn't make too much of keeping it. At the same time, it is important to ensure that it doesn't become part of larger pattern of dishonesty. Keeping the money can be fun. It is such a small sum (not like the $10,000 the cabby found). Irma's pocketing the money is mischief that does little harm, like a minor practical joke. It will hardly be noticed by anyone. A small blot is, after all, a little color on what might otherwise be a monochromatic righteousness. The moralistic are often insufferable bores.

Nevertheless, naughtiness has a way of becoming nastiness, and mischief turns into malice. So while it may not be like putting a drop of poison into a well, it could turn into a slippery slope, or the camel's nose under the tent. We think we can control ourselves but find that we go faster and faster downhill until we are in the pit of immorality. Or we let the camel stick its nose where it doesn't belong and the next thing we know, the smelly creature is standing in our living room.

It may be that if we do something small, we begin to rationalize and lose track of what it is to be honest, until we could no longer be honest if we tried.

# 24

# Should I Be Free to Choose All My Associations?

Kimberly shows up at tryouts for an all-boy basketball team in a privately sponsored league. The coach agrees that she is one of the best players. Two of the star athletes on the team say they will quit if Kimberly is allowed to play with them. The coach decides not to put her on the team, claiming that her presence would be disruptive and impractical. He has found that when a girl (cheerleader or manager) travels with the team, the boys are rowdy and have difficulty concentrating on the game. The coach also says that locker room space would be impossible to get at most gyms, since visiting teams already use the girls' locker room. Furthermore, the team wouldn't be as competitive without the two boys.

Some questions to ask yourself:

1. Do people have a right to associate with whomever they wish?
2. Does the right to free association apply to groups as well as individuals?

3. Should one sex be allowed to exclude another from its activities?
4. Do the boys have a right to refuse to play with a girl?
5. Are the boys morally right?
6. Is the coach doing the right thing?

## The Problem: Choosing Your Friends versus Not Discriminating

Written into the Bill of Rights is the freedom of assembly. Without compelling social purpose, the government can't prevent people from gathering together as they want. What constitutes compelling social purpose is often the sticking point. A colleague was once sitting in a car talking to a friend when the police threatened to arrest him if he didn't move on. Hugh thought that the reason for such a demand was that he was black and his car was parked in an all-white, wealthy, suburban neighborhood. "Racial profiling"—that is, contending that particular racial groups are more likely to commit crimes than others—isn't a compelling reason. Hugh had a right to be where he wanted, and the government didn't have the right to make him move.

But what about the other side of the coin? Does the government have the right to force us to associate with people not of our own choosing? What kind of freedom could we claim if we couldn't choose our own associates, acquaintances, or friends?

## Why Free Association Is Important

Once I visited a commune in Connecticut, staying for nearly two weeks. This community, built upon principles of nonviolence, cooperation, and social justice, supported itself by manufacturing children's toys at its own factory. Everyone worked, including those who were physically or mentally challenged. No one received a salary. Instead, the commune provided for all the amenities, from housing to clothing, from entertainment to education, distributing the goods equally among all.

Children were raised in this noncompetitive atmosphere. They attended their own school on the commune and participated in doing the chores from a very early age. Sharing and concern for others were primary values. They did their best not to hurt one another's feelings. They showed extraordinary kindness toward each other.

One afternoon after work hours, I saw a couple of teenage boys from the commune playing basketball. I went to join them. The boys weren't very good, so I helped them practice a bit, then suggested that we play a two-on-one—both of them against me. Of course, they let me take out the ball first. I drove to the basket; they stepped aside. So we stopped play and I coached them on defensive skills. Then they took out the ball, passed to each other. When I moved up on them to stop them from driving to the basket or to block their shot, they were flustered and as much as handed the ball to me, as if to say, "Here, you want it so badly, you can have it. You just have to ask."

This was the most peculiar basketball game I've ever played. I wanted to win, but they just wanted to share; I wanted a good competitive game, they wanted to cooperate.

I left shaking my head. The boys (I can't call them my competitors) were probably shaking theirs as well. We were playing the same game but with different purposes, different values, and different meanings. What gave me enjoyment gave them cause for concern. But I couldn't enjoy the game if no one challenged me.

I remembered this experience as I thought about this vignette. The basic issue for me is whether people have the right to associate with whomever they want and to establish whatever rules they want to govern themselves. The commune's unwritten values were cooperation, inclusiveness regardless of one's ability, and not hurting anyone's feelings. Society at large doesn't abide by these values, but the commune is free to go its own way, imparting its own ideology, educating its children in its own way of life. The U.S. Supreme Court said basically the same thing about the Boy Scouts and homosexuals. Since the Boy Scouts is a private organization, the Court reasoned, it is free to make its own rules and if it wanted to bar homosexuals, then that is its right.

## Distinguishing between Legal and Moral Rights

With these thoughts in mind, let's look at the situation of Kimberly. Here there is also a group that wants things its own way. Boys want to play with boys and only boys, and this appears to be supported by the larger community. The boys don't want a girl on the team and are willing to quit the league in order to keep things as they are. They, like the boys on the commune I visited, have a value that is more important than winning. In this case the value isn't sparing Kimberly's feelings, but male bonding.

I'd like to approach Kimberly's situation in terms of right of association. And I want to consider it mainly from the point of view of the coach's actions rather than the boys' wishes, since the coach serves as the society's surrogate and the resolution of the conflict ought to proceed from a mature point of view.

One solution to this dilemma may be legal. If the basketball team is in some way government funded, then there may be real legal issues. To exclude someone who is otherwise qualified from the team because of her sex when that same team is subsidized by taxpayer money is unconstitutional. If that's all there were to the situation, there wouldn't be much to discuss. But more interesting moral issues arise here because this is a private league. So, for the sake of this discussion, I want to assume that there are no legal or constitutional considerations, and instead I want to answer the question not as a lawyer but as a moral philosopher.

The coach believes that accepting the girl would endanger the team's chances of winning, because Kimberly's presence would be disruptive. He thinks that no matter how stunning Kimberly's athletic abilities, she would still be a liability, and he would lose more than he would gain. I don't know what the coach thinks of girls. You don't have to assume that he is a sexist to deny Kimberly a place, only that he is convinced that the point of coaching a team is to win as many games as possible. Operating under that premise, the coach is right in contending that he is under no obligation to accept anyone who tries out, no matter how skilled they may be. He can take only those who he thinks will contribute to the team's overall production. There's more to winning than talent, as many frustrated coaches know. A team needs players who also fit in; basketball is, after all, a team sport.

So even if Kimberly were the best player to step onto the court in decades, the coach could, with good reason, reject her. Kimberly is rejected not because of what she does but because of the reactions of others to her. If Kimberly were a selfish player, she could learn how to be a cooperative teammate; if she didn't get along well with others, she could learn how not to irritate. But a girl cannot learn to become a boy. There is nothing that Kimberly can do to satisfy the objections of the boys. Her problem is her anatomy, not her personality or her skills. She has done all in her power to qualify for the team.

## Private versus Public Groups

Some might argue that the boys have the right not to play with girls if they don't want to. By way of analogy, they might say that if the hypothetical Albanian Fraternal basketball team turned away the greatest athlete, it would be understandable and correct if the person wasn't Albanian. The purpose of such a team is not simply to win its games but to win its games as Albanians. The club's purpose is primarily to foster ethnic identity, and it plays its games within that context.

This is true enough. But the team described in this vignette is different. It is community-based and is tolerated and maybe even supported by the community because it serves the general interests of the community. If a community supports organized sports, it does so in the service of certain values. After all, why would the community support an activity except to accomplish or promote some goal? For the Aztecs, for example, sports were in the service of religion; for the late nineteenth-century British, sports were used to develop superior soldiers. In the United States today, several reasons are offered regarding the value of organized physical activity. Among them are that it helps promote self-confidence and good character. We think that it's good for children to be engaged in sports because we think that they will learn the values of compassion, fairness, integrity, and what researchers David Shields and Brenda Bredemeir call "sportspersonship."

Whether physical activities actually produce these qualities is open to question. But society thinks they do and they ought to. It is hard to see how discrimination against a class of people fosters those values. To reject Kimberly is to contradict, at the least, the value of fairness. Of course, this is not the only value a community may want to promote. But it does seem to me to be a correct ethical one. Turning Kimberly away, rather than educating the boys as to treating everyone fairly, is to miss part of the point of playing.

# Confronting Stereotypes and Prejudice

I asked George Vecsey what he thought about this situation, since he is a sports columnist with the *New York Times* and has daughters who were student athletes. In addition, Vecsey was the religion editor of the *Times* before moving over to sports.

"The core of the problem—a girl wanting to play with the boys—sounds as real and immediate as when my children, now adults, were coming along. My older daughter played in girls' leagues when they were available, but was good enough and competitive enough that she wanted to play against boys," Vecsey says. "There was a summer Police Athletic League softball program that was used by boys only. My daughter, then around twelve or thirteen, asked to play, and was told she could. Several boys voiced their unhappiness, but basically she was on the team."

Vecsey continues, "At the age of, let's say nine, there are certainly more important lessons than winning or losing. The elders surely have the right to make decisions for children of that age. I would like to think that adults would accept the right (or desire) of a girl to compete—particularly if there were no comparable level of competition for a girl."

At a later age, the situation may be slightly different. Vecsey says, "The question could be asked of the children: If Kimberly is good enough to play, who is really threatened—the two superior male athletes who are talking about quitting, or the boy who might play a little less because the girl took his spot on the starting team? What's really the issue? Let everybody talk. They just might work it out. At any rate, I would advise Kimberly's family to pursue her participation. In the long run, I see no negatives to having a girl play at Little League age—and I see considerable positives in forcing boys to face some of the old stereotypes. And I recall the bottom line in the community program I ran in my town: if a parent or child could not live up to rules against cursing or heckling or rough play, they were invited to leave. I have seen our commissioner tell a father to go home from a game because he was yelling at his own son. The man left and never came back. The community had given the commissioner these powers. In the long run, the 'community' of this basketball program could rule that a girl is welcome to compete."

## Inclusiveness versus Winning at All Costs

Places on this team ought to be distributed on the basis of what each has earned compared to the performance of others. For a team such as this one, the only relevant consideration for membership is the ability to play basketball. Using this standard for fairness, Kimberly has outperformed others and therefore deserves a place on the team. The treatment she receives is undeserved and affects her adversely. Kimberly is denied a place on the team solely on the basis of her being female. No other relevant characteristic of hers contributed to her rejection. Ethical concerns lead us toward inclusiveness rather than exclusiveness, separateness, and privilege. It is incumbent upon those who discriminate against classes of individuals to justify their actions on the basis of an ethical principle. Winning over all doesn't meet the test of ethical acceptability.

Kimberly has done nothing to warrant such treatment. The attitudes of others make her sex a liability. While the boys' ability to concentrate on the game may be impaired by her presence, it is the boys' attitudes that need addressing. Vecsey agrees. "Kimberly's family probably pays taxes or dues or church tithes to support this league. They have the right to pursue her hopes of playing in this league presumably near her home. She and her family should lobby with community leaders—elected officials, recreation officials, school officials, coaches, whatever. Ask for some kind of structured meeting or hearing—with the objecting boys present, along with some peers and some responsible adults, but not a general "town meeting," which could be counter-productive. Somebody just might raise the point with the boys: Is playing against a girl in this local league going to keep them from the National Basketball Association? Is it going to cost them a college scholarship? It doesn't sound that way."

## Not Blaming the Victim

Kimberly suffers because of some anticipated effect upon team play. Let's say that some leave the team because of her, let's say that her playing on the team distracts others—this isn't enough to prevent Kimberly from playing. She isn't at fault. It is the attitudes of others that are at fault. She shouldn't have to pay for what others do.

The matter of not having a locker room available for Kimberly strikes me as a rationalization, a grasping at straws to cover the discrimination. Vecsey agrees. "I'm sure that is true at many gyms and schools and clubs. It is also true that young men socialize in the locker room, sharing secrets and lies and boasts, and they probably need and deserve some of these rites. But you can't tell me there are not ways around the shower and bathroom issues. A fading minority of professional athletes still grumble about female sportswriters in the locker room. The answer: a towel and a bathrobe. That simple."

Vecsey continues, "The fact is, many high school athletes encounter female managers, female trainers, female doctors, female coaches, female administrators, female journalists, maybe even female officials, and soon come to regard them as part of the process. Special arrangements are possible at some gyms; she could use the locker room before or after the boys; she may arrive wearing her sneakers and shorts and choose not take a shower afterward. Kimberly may decide that these alternatives are too embarrassing and decide not to continue playing, but that is her choice to make."

## Real Differences Really Matter

By denying Kimberly the chance to play on the team because others have trouble with her being a girl, the coach is reacting much like the military before segregation was overturned in the armed forces. Racially mixing the troops, part of the argument against integration went, would lower the morale of the whites and therefore affect the ability of the military to carry out its mission. Not everyone agreed. In July 1948, President Harry Truman ordered the integration of the armed forces. (We now know from his staff papers that the president was moved as much by a desire to have black support for the upcoming election as by the desire to act ethically. Not all right actions need to be motivated by purely moral reasons.)

Today the military is the paragon of racial fairness. If whites couldn't—wouldn't—mix with blacks, then it was incumbent upon the armed services to redress the racism, not give in to it. However, for some, it is easier to continue to discriminate than to rectify the ethical violation. Blacks upset whites? Keep blacks out. Girls upset boys? Don't allow girls in. Gays upset straight people? Keep them in the closet.

Having said this, there may be times in which it is better to separate males and females. That is the conclusion of some branches of the military today. After years of sex-integrated basic training, the armed services are moving toward sex-segregated training, as has always been the case for the Marines. This move can be seen as different from merely resegregating the troops. The separate training isn't being implemented because males object to having women around, but because women can get better training by being in all-female companies at this stage of their career. The new direction isn't to mollify the sexism of the male soldiers but to better serve the female soldiers. The armed services tried to eradicate harassment of women, but failed in basic training. The point of the segregation is to make them better soldiers, better able to compete in the long run, to create a more equitable military culture.

This is much the same rationale as having all-women colleges or all-black colleges. Some women and blacks, it is claimed, perform better in an environment that supports their intellectual talents, where they needn't deal with biases and a style of intellectualism that favors males or whites.

"By the teenage years," Vecsey says, "there are reasonably fast leagues for the bigger, faster, stronger, more aggressive male athletes. I would argue that mixing girls and boys might hold back the development of the better athletes." Vecsey gives the example of Nancy Lieberman-Kline, who became a professional basketball player. "Nancy used to ride the subways of New York City from her home in Far Rockaway to the playgrounds of Harlem, to find competition against the best male players. The men in Harlem called her 'Fire,' and not just because of her red hair, either. She sought out the best levels. She found a way. I think girls will continue to seek out the best competition. Fortunately, more and more is available to women."

## Unfair Discrimination

But this still doesn't fully address Kimberly's problem. She wants to play on this team, not another; she is as qualified as any male. No one is giving her anything.

"It might be helpful for trained leaders (teacher, clergy, coach, social workers, counselors) to hold a group session, bringing the children together to discuss the agendas, overt and hidden," Vecsey says. "At that point, it might be determined whether it is really the two boys who object, or whether it is a parent still operating on feelings from an era when girls did not try to compete. I would think it more productive to limit the meeting to the children. Quite often, adults speaking their piece in large communal meetings are not a pretty sight. However, if the group sentiment went against her, Kimberly might ask if she wants to associate with that attitude in the first place. I would urge her to look harder for a high level of girls' competition. These days it is not impossible to find. We have, indeed, come a long way."

Vecsey's suggestion is a practical one. It may be the only solution for Kimberly, but it is a solution that is rooted in an unethical situation. The burden here shouldn't be on Kimberly. I think that she should have the chance to play on the team whatever the group sentiment. The only moral course is one that allows qualified players on the team, even if it means losing other players and a championship. Some things are more important than winning. Being fair is one of them.

## 25

Does It Matter What I Buy?

The Wallaces live on a tight budget. They are very careful how they spend their money, often forgoing luxuries so they can save for their future. After years of coaxing, their old car is finally ready to give out. Mr. Wallace can't do any more to save it.

They check consumer magazines and find that foreign cars are more reliable and better built than American cars. In the long run they are cheaper to own than domestic cars. They are also more efficient and therefore less polluting. However, the Wallaces want to support American workers and believe that people should be willing to make sacrifices to support their fellow citizens. They decide to buy a Chevrolet.

Some questions to ask yourself:

1. Are your purchases made solely on the basis of whether you want or need the item?
2. Is it important to know who made what you buy and under what circumstances they were made?
3. Should you balance concerns for the welfare of others with your desire to get the best buy for your money?

4. Should ethical considerations play a role in purchasing an item?

5. Are the Wallaces making the right moral choice?

# The Problem:
## Considering Myself versus Considering Others I May Not Even Know

The Wallace family is fictitious, but I know people like them. They are concerned about the impact their spending will have on others and the environment. Most of my students, though, think this anecdote is pure fantasy. For them it's ludicrous, completely alien. No one ever makes such a decision. The only interest for the Wallaces, they say, is getting the best deal for their money. It isn't so much that they disagree with the Wallaces' decision as that they don't recognize that there are choices at all. To them it's like being offered a week at the Hilton on the beach in Hawaii or an overnight stay in a fleabag hotel in a run-down neighborhood in a boring city.

As long as our purchases are legal, we have met the moral standard, many people say. This is what consumer capitalism is all about. This understanding may meet the standards of economists, but a different standard is used by those concerned with ethics.

## Preferences, Prudence, and Ethics:
### Do I Like It? Can I Afford It? Is It Right?

Let's take a closer look at the ethics of buying. In addition to wanting something is the matter of whether we can afford it. If I don't buy my child her needed school supplies because I've spent everything on CDs, this certainly would have to be morally dubious. What I buy has to be looked at in relation to other things I need to buy. So the first step for the Wallaces is to look at their fixed and anticipated expenses, decide what is discretionary spending and what is a necessity, then make a list of priorities about how to spend their discretionary money. Perhaps taking a long-needed vacation is more important than getting a new car, in which case they will make do a little longer with the old car. Or maybe the new car is the thing they want most, and they can afford it, so they go shopping.

Mostly I buy something because I think I need it one way or another. When I spend a lot of money, I pause, trying to distinguish between actually needing something and simply wanting it. Will I have to give up something else if I buy it? After assuring myself that I am truly going to purchase it, I then want to know if I am getting the best buy for my money. For a car, I will do comparison shopping, ask some friends if they are pleased with their cars, read a few auto magazines, and consult *Consumer Reports.*

Up until this point, my interests are preferential and prudential and to a smaller extent moral. However, beyond asking myself, "Do I like it?" and "Can I afford it?" loom largely ethical considerations. These are real, even if hidden, because we live in a world with other people and our actions affect them. Other people have an interest in what we do with our money to the extent their lives are affected by the decisions we make. So even if I were superwealthy and took no more notice of spending $50,000 than 50¢, it is still an ethically questionable purchase.

One example is pretty straightforward. We all breathe the same air. Fuel-inefficient cars pollute the air. It is wrong to poison someone else. Therefore, keeping the air clean is a moral issue. As a society, we have recognized that we can't rely solely on individuals to buy fuel-efficient cars, so we have laws that force car manufacturers to sell cars that get higher miles per gallon, while simultaneously outlawing the sale of leaded gas.

## How the Desire for Profits Can Benefit Many

In today's world, market values often supersede ethical values. When was the last time you saw a political talk show that had an ethicist and an economist discussing policy issues? The popularity of the accounting term the *bottom line* in everyday conversation shows just how far-reaching a business mentality has become. Adam Smith's philosophy, in its popular and misunderstood form in which greed is good, has the upper hand, even among those who are not businesspeople. Producers' and consumers' philosophies are alike: as long as wealth is not obtained through fraud or force, it is morally acceptable. The ethical businessperson does not lie, cheat, coerce, or break the law. That's all that is morally required. Anything more is naive, unrealistic, and hopelessly idealistic, it is often said.

Smith's views have been taken to mean that self-interest is in itself moral, since the cumulative effect of increased production benefits everyone in the long run. Smith didn't claim that selfishness was good (or that benevolence was bad) but that acting on self-interest led to something good. He approved of acting on self-interest not because he favored individualism or consumerism. He favored capitalism because he believed that making a profit is a better way to help people get what they want than by giving them what you think they need.

For Smith, self-interest and the common good were not at odds, since one led to the other. He encouraged the pursuit of self-interest because it created a greater common good. But things don't always work out for the best. The manufacture and sale of child pornography and handguns to children are two examples. I'm not talking about laws, but morality here.

## How the Desire to Consume May Harm Others

Now let's look at consumption rather than production. What is the larger good to which self-interested buying relates? Producers can at least say that they make no judgments about what they produce. Let the consumer decide if their product is worthy. If no one wants their goods, they will go bankrupt. If, on the other hand, people buy what they have to sell, they are enhancing the freedom of choice.

What good, other than individual satisfaction, is enhanced by consumption guided only by prudence? That answer depends upon what is purchased, under what conditions, and from whom. For example, there is a delicatessen in my neighborhood that, along with cold cuts and soda, sells several newspapers. A number of years ago a customer noticed that the German-language newspaper sold there was noted for its anti-Semitism. When the owner refused to remove the offending paper, the customer decided to find another store to buy his lunches. Although it was more costly in terms of time and money to go to another deli for similar sandwiches and chips, the patron put his money where his mouth was, so to speak. He didn't want his money supporting a cause that he despised, even though it cost him extra.

## Choosing to Not Aid the Immoral

When the issue is local and involves small sums of money or when it is easy to find an alternative, the dilemma may be easy to resolve.

But it is more difficult if the cost to us is high. Then we balance the price against how important the issue is to us. In the above example, eating roast beef sandwiches and potato salad isn't important, it is easy to give up. If another delicatessen is nearby, it is easy for the customer to boycott the store he doesn't like. But if he loves deli sandwiches and they can't be gotten elsewhere, then it is harder. Still, if anti-Semitism is abhorrent, then the committed person would be willing to forgo all the pleasures and suffer the pain.

Each purchase we make involves the same considerations, at some level, as the deli boycott. Every time we spend money, someone benefits from it. Do we want to support this person? Does our money go to something we find repugnant? Socially conscious spending takes into account the policies of those who sell to us. Everything being equal, it is better to reward decent people by supporting them through our purchases than it is to buy the same thing from a bunch of gangsters. Just as it is wrong to buy a stolen jacket at a discount price, it is wrong to put our money into the hands of those who use it in ways we consider unethical.

When the Wallaces decide to buy an American car instead of the better-value foreign make, they determine that they are willing to personally subsidize American workers. They believe, I guess, that U.S. workers will lose their jobs unless they—and other Americans—are willing to buy the cars made in the United States, even when it means making a sacrifice.

I asked philosopher David Sprintzen what he thought of the hypothetical Wallaces' decision. Sprintzen teaches at C.W. Post College and is also the founder of the Long Island Progressive Coalition. "The Wallaces deserve respect for their sensitivity and willingness to make a personal sacrifice on their behalf." Both Sprinzten and I admire the Wallaces' desire to look at how their purchases affect others. It is a morally worthy view, revealing a philosophy that recognizes that real satisfaction resides elsewhere than in selfishness and self-centeredness. Their willingness to make sacrifices to help others is noble.

## The Importance of Loyalty

But is it ethical to support Americans rather than those from elsewhere? "All people have an equal right to decent conditions of life, both economic, political, and social," Sprintzen says. "They have an equal right to a decent job at a family-supporting wage. But it doesn't follow that each of us has an equal obligation to contribute equally to everyone's well-being. You must not directly harm another, or knowingly contribute to their degradation. But you are not, and cannot, be held responsible for all of the indirect consequences of our actions—for they are ultimately infinite and unknowable. Nor are you completely responsible for the institutions that determine the relation between our actions and their worldwide consequences. Our moral responsibility to others must be proportional both to our institutional connection with them and to the levers of influence that are available to us," Sprintzen continues. "Our responsibility is far greater toward those who are directly bound up with us in organized communities, second only to our responsibility to and for those with whom you have direct face-to-face personal relations. Loyalty is a product of such personal interactions. A coherent community life is vital to personal integrity and moral action. It is precisely this dynamic that provides the moral and political justification for the Wallaces' concern for the jobs of American workers. You are bound up with our fellow Americans in an effective political community for the success of which you bear a level of moral responsibility commensurate with our ability to maintain or transform the relevant institutions of production and distribution. It follows that American workers have a legitimate and strong claim on our concern and action."

# Loyalty in Conflict with Principles

Socrates addresses a similar question in "Euthyphro." Here a son is in court to argue against his father for causing the death of a slave. The ancient philosopher doesn't address the question directly, but implies that being loyal to one's parent is more important than adhering to an ideal, such as applying justice blindly, simply because custom or the gods or the law tells us that is how it should be. Contemporary philosopher Henry Louis Gates Jr. makes a similar case when he urges people to consider loyalty over principle.

I agree with Gates, to a point. I suppose it is the same point that was reached by David Kaczynski when, after much agonizing, he decided to turn in his brother Ted to the FBI as the Unabomber suspect. Preventing the future deaths of strangers was more important than keeping his brother out of prison. We build our sense of ethics from the inside out, as it were. We begin with particular—people we know, who know us, who have taken care of us, those closest to us—and move to the general, namely, neighbors and on to still larger circles. Loyalty to the local doesn't trump everything, though. It functions much like confidentiality. There is a presumption in favor of it, but sometimes other matters are more important.

# Finding the Facts and Making an Educated Guess

In judging the Wallaces' impulse to help their fellow citizens, we need to consider the factors. The road to hell, after all, is paved with good intentions. Sprintzen thinks that their decision fails at this point. "The Wallaces might feel righteous in sacrificing on behalf of their fellow citizens," he says, "but I am highly dubious about the political significance, and hence the real moral value, of the politics of 'bearing witness' or of 'moral purity.' A moral action that is unlikely to have the intended moral consequences is not only ineffective, it may be even worse. It may give the illusion of effectiveness, and a feeling of self-righteous satisfaction, while avoiding, or even worse, detracting from those efforts that offer a real chance of making a significant difference in the lives of those affected."

I disagree. Bearing witness may or may not be an effective tool for social change. Others who know the Wallaces may pause and think about their own behavior. The Wallaces' example may inspire others to decide to take action in their own lives, even leading some to join social cause organizations. Sometimes it is the act of one person that precipitates a social movement. And, finally, it's just as likely that the Wallaces' decision will direct them to take further action as it is that it will deflect them from doing something more effective. The "slippery slope" argument can be used here, but in reverse: instead of leading down the road to perdition, a certain action can lead to more critical moral thinking and more effective change.

Aside from these speculative considerations, the Wallaces should do a little more research. If buying the best car isn't the prime consideration, then they should also consider another set of questions: Which corporation really helps its labor force, which is most concerned about the environment, which is community-minded, what kinds of other products does the company make? There is also the complicated question regarding which car is really an American car. Is it one made in the United States, even though the corporation may be foreign? What about the reverse, when the car is made by a U.S. corporation but in a foreign country? The answers to these and similar questions can be found in any local library.

The Wallaces also need to balance two competing ethical claims:

loyalty against consideration for the environment. If buying an American car means keeping someone employed at the expense of someone else's health, what should they decide?

The fundamental point in the Wallaces' story is that our money serves larger causes, and the way in which we spend our money reveals our commitments and values. I agree with the Buddhist philosopher Thich Nhat Hanh, who implores us to keep a careful awareness of what we consume. The ethical perspective examines the use of money in light of the best way of promoting our basic values. Loyalty must be a basic value. It is the fundamental commitment that follows from caring about people.

# 26

❧

# Do I Confront People about Their Habits or What They Wear?

Martin brings his good friend Cindy to his church. She quickly becomes an active member and works on several committees. She also joins Martin's social circle.

Everyone likes Cindy, except for one problem. She always wears perfume that some describe as overpowering and others as cloying. A few say the smell makes them choke and they have to stay on the other side of the room when she is present.

One member has come to the minister to tell him that she can't do her volunteer work any longer because Cindy has joined them in a small, unventilated room. She asks the minister to tell Cindy to stop using the perfume.

The minister talks to Cindy one morning after services to tell her that she can no longer wear her perfume to church because it is driving other people away.

Some questions to ask yourself:

1. Does anyone have the right to tell you what to wear?
2. What do you do when you encounter someone offensive?
3. Does it matter how well you know the person?

4. How do you balance the rights of an individual with the needs of the group?
5. Is the minister doing the right thing?

# The Problem:
## Pleasing Yourself versus Pleasing Others

The problem here is that we all have to live with other people. If we lived by ourselves, we could do whatever we want. One of life's major problems is how to take care of ourselves and at the same time be considerate of other people. Occasionally this isn't a problem at all but one of life's blessings. We want to give to others, we enjoy being generous, we take pleasure in helping another succeed. We become better people as we help others find the best in themselves.

But other times we find ourselves in conflict. What we want isn't what someone else wants. It's a kind of zero-sum game in which one person comes out ahead only at the other's expense. Matters of justice frequently fall into this category.

In this story, though, the stakes aren't so lofty. This is a matter of personal taste. Yet the vignette does raise a basic question about the rights of an individual.

Does an irritation rise to the level of a moral offense, or should individuals be free to do as they please in terms of grooming?

# Two Kinds of Freedom:
## Freedom To and Freedom From

Once I was on a committee with a woman who chain-smoked. At first a few people asked her not to smoke during the meeting. She refused, staking her moral claim to a right to smoke. No one had a right to tell her what to do, any more than they had the right to tell her what to say. Over time more people asked her not to smoke in their presence, and tempers spilled over. She remained angry and continued to claim it was her right to smoke, but grudgingly, as the social pressure mounted, she left the room whenever she wanted to light up.

Few fight over smoking in public nowadays. Today people who dislike smoking can retreat from personal confrontations by pointing to the regulations against smoking in public places and by justifying their stance by citing studies that claim that secondhand smoke is harmful. It isn't any longer a clash of two moral rights, but a matter of public health.

Smoking versus no smoking was a classic case of two kinds of freedom: the freedom *to smoke* and the freedom *from smoke*. Similar types of conflict can arise in the business world, where on one side owners say, "I have the right to run my business as I please," and on the other side workers or the public counter with, "I have a right to be safe."

Sometimes it is the government itself that is up against citizens, as when an old garbage dump is filled and a new one needs to be opened somewhere, somehow.

## Harm versus Taste

Many conflicts of ours fall into a gray zone. What someone does isn't directly harmful to other people, but some are sensitive and find what he does objectionable. A dress code is an example of this. Some school districts allow female teachers to wear sandals but bar male teachers from wearing sandals. A man, but not a woman, can walk shirtless on the street, although many people consider it tasteless. Acceptable and morally approved modes of dress are ever shifting and often culturally specific. For example, in Rio de Janeiro, pedestrians stroll on the most sophisticated streets wearing bathing suits, while today in the United States some states allow women to be bare-breasted on the beaches, though it is still a rare event where families are present.

Even as some social constraints fall away, new fences are erected around old habits. Moral outrage over drunk driving led to new regulations for drinking and driving. ("I have the right to get drunk" lost the argument with "I have a right not to be killed by someone out of control.")

New York became the first state in the country to ban talking on hand-held cell phones while driving. The arguments were the same as those around drinking and driving. This leads many to ask, "Where will this end? Will it be made a crime to listen to the radio or talk to another passenger or blow my nose while driving?"

Where do we draw the line? Ideally, we would all do what we want all the time. But the ideal world isn't the real world. There's nothing wrong with doing whatever we want, as long as we don't hurt anyone. But actions do have consequences. If I were a hermit, it wouldn't matter where I smoked. If cars were on automatic pilot so they could never crash, it wouldn't matter if I was blotto when I stepped behind the wheel, nor would it make a difference if I developed cauliflower ear from too much time on the phone. But cigarette smoke harms and drunk drivers kill, and one of the requirements of morality is that we do no harm, if at all possible.

But what about those things that don't really harm others, but only make them uncomfortable?

# Your Problem versus Someone Else's Problem

Someone once quipped that my freedom ends at the tip of your nose. That literally seems to be what's at issue in this vignette.

The problem between Cindy and others appears similar to the disagreement between smokers and antismokers. However, there is a major difference. Cindy's acquaintances simply don't like the way she smells. They may find it unpleasant or even offensive. But they are not claiming that it makes them sick. No one is being harmed.

In another way, though, it is very much like the smoking/no smoking argument, at least in the stages before it was known to be a medical matter. The antismokers said, "The smoke stinks and I don't want to be around it." So it's a matter of preference.

"You don't like it that I smoke? Then don't come to the meeting," colleagues said.

"I have as much right to be at this meeting as you," another said. "So don't smoke or else stay home."

This reminds me of my Parmesan cheese dilemma. I can't stand the smell. Other people wouldn't dream of eating some Italian food without it. I don't tell them to stop using the cheese. Instead, I try to stay out of pizza parlors. When I can't escape and find myself sitting next to someone whose food is full of the cheese, I try to move to the other end of the table. I don't tell anyone what to order, but I do try to avoid putting myself in the situation. I recognize it as my problem and take responsibility for finding a solution that doesn't impose my quirk on other people.

## Being Honest with Others

Most of the time, I don't tell others what bothers me. But sometimes not explaining what bothers us can mean the end of a relationship. This is what happened to Hans Christian Andersen when he visited Charles Dickens in England. Andersen didn't know when to leave. For five weeks he made himself at home. When he left, Dickens put up a card that read, "Hans Andersen slept in this room for five weeks—which seemed to the family ages!" Dickens had nothing to do with Andersen after that and Andersen never understood what had happened.

Just imagine what would happen if everyone who was bothered by Cindy's perfume took the same tack as Dickens did with Andersen. People would avoid her. She would end up sitting by herself in the pew; at socials she would be on one side of the room and everyone else on another. She would no longer receive invitations to events and, like Andersen, she wouldn't have a clue why. All this because no one would talk to her.

There's a double hurt here. On the one hand, she would be ostracized, the modern equivalent of a shunning. On the other hand, the church would be hurt, as participation would fall off as people stayed away just to avoid being in Cindy's presence.

## The One versus the Many

So for the sake of both Cindy and the church, it is best if she is talked to. She needs to be told that her perfume is causing a problem. It is because harm is being done that the situation needs attention. It's too much to hope that it will somehow take care of itself. But who should talk to her, and what precisely should Cindy be told?

Most people would agree that if a person disrupts a church service, the church should put a stop to it. After all, people come to church for a particular purpose. If someone shouts in the middle of silent prayer, she would be shushed. If she praised Jesus in a synagogue, she might be asked to leave. If she ate a sardine sandwich during worship hour, she might be told that eating isn't allowed.

Every organization has the right to its own integrity and to define acceptable rules of behavior. The difficulty is finding the balance between quirkiness of an individual with the needs of the group not to be unduly bothered. Philosophers call this the problem of the one and the many. A group that regulates all personal behavior is disrespectful of the individual; individuals who disregard the wishes of others are disrespectful of the group.

It is a thin line between coercion of the person on the one side and disintegration of the group on the other. In this particular case, Cindy has a right to know why others are avoiding her.

## Avoiding Embarrassing
## Another in Public

I asked Michael Katz, a congregational rabbi, what he thought should be done.

"Foremost is the concern that someone not be embarrassed in public. So one response is to have a discussion about the needs of individuals among us. Let's discuss and develop a general policy with respect to the sensitivities and needs of everyone. This way the issue becomes one of principle, and one of accommodating the needs of individuals in our midst, rather than how to control Cindy."

Katz continues by offering an alternative. The minister can speak privately to Cindy and convey the following: " 'We have a member (no names) who has a problem—severe allergic reaction to perfume. She was embarrassed to come to you directly and talk to you, because your perfume seems to affect her and she doesn't want to offend you. The issue is her allergy, not your grooming habits. She would be eternally grateful if you could accommodate her needs.' While this may not be 100 percent true—the problem is Cindy's grooming habits—we are permitted to tell a white lie in order to avoid embarrassment and humiliation to another."

I agree with Katz that not embarrassing people, especially in public, is an important value. It is related to a basic principle in ethics, mainly respect for people. For this reason, bending the truth for the sake of peace can sometimes be considered. To adhere to truth-telling under all circumstances can be cruel.

## White Lies May Help or They May Hurt

I'm not sure this is one of those instances, although it may turn out to be. In my experience, I find that many people will choose to avoid what they think will be confrontation. They are so afraid of disrupting a relationship or creating bad feelings, they will resort to white lies. Such lies—"social lubricants," someone once called them—are all too often used as an excuse to avoid the harder task of speaking honestly but with sensitivity. If the problem really is Cindy's grooming, then that should be stated in a way that isn't harsh or embarrassing. Everyone has a right to accurate information about herself. Human dignity is associated with freedom of choice. So one really can't be a free person if she is kept in the dark or if what she is told isn't true. Cindy is being patronized and therefore disrespected if she is told a white lie. It's as though she isn't strong enough to handle the truth. I've been forced into telling white lies. This has been when someone has asked me something about another individual that was none of his business. This was gossip and prying.

If Cindy isn't told the truth, she may not wear the perfume to church but continue to put it on when she goes elsewhere. She will meet with the same results. She will learn nothing from the white lie because she hasn't been given the opportunity to learn the real facts involved.

The question is how to approach Cindy is such a way that it won't create more harm than good. As Katz says, "This is certainly a Jewish approach, based upon the verse in the Torah, 'You shall surely rebuke/reprove your fellow, but bear no guilt,' which is interpreted by the rabbis as: Confront them about issues that are troubling, but do it in a way that causes no more harm. And every clergyperson would agree that it is unfair to put the minister into the role of group policeman. (Yet, if it is determined that the other congregants are merely being priggish and that they, not Cindy, are the real problem, then the minister will have to act as policeman.)"

The right person to address Cindy's problem is Martin, the one closest to her. So the minister should turn the matter over to Martin. But if Martin doesn't understand the issue or refuses, then it is proper for the minister to talk to Cindy, for he has the obligation to care for the entire congregation.

We don't know from the information given whether the minister presents an ultimatum to Cindy. It may be that even with all the minister's great pastoral and persuasive skills, Cindy refuses to tone down her perfume. Then the minister needs to make a judgment. Is Cindy the source of the problem? She may be engaged in a harmless exercise in self-expression. Or are the complainers the real problem? They may be priggish, as pointed out by Katz.

The temptation is great to do a crude calculation and decide who contributes the most to the church. If Cindy works hard and makes a large pledge, the minister may be seduced into siding with her. Or conversely, if the complainers are big contributors, he might give them more weight. While this can't be completely discounted, it must remain only one consideration.

## The Reasonable Person Guide

Here the minister may use the yardstick that is employed by justices, the reasonable person guide. How would a reasonable person react to Cindy's perfume? How would a reasonable person judge the objections to her wearing perfume?

The situation is different if, in fact, someone gets sick from Cindy's perfume. Then the issue is closer to that of smoking. Here Cindy's desire to smell a certain way isn't as important as the health of another individual. A real difficulty, however, is deciding whether someone truly is allergic or if she is exaggerating as a method of getting her own way.

One can imagine many other possibilities in this vignette. For this reason, it is a good example of the need to understand the facts and to figure out who has an interest and what is the best way of handling the problem.

# How Responsible
# Should I Be?

One Thursday afternoon at about 2:30, Raymond parks
his car next to a county truck. As he leaves his car, he notes
that two county uniformed workers are asleep in the cab.
When Raymond returns more than an hour and a half later,
the truck is parked in the same place and the two employees are still asleep. He decides to report the incident to the
county department.

Some questions to ask yourself:

1. What obligations do you have to the community?
2. Do you have a right to make sure that your tax dollars are
   used properly?
3. Do you have a responsibility to do something when you
   think public money is being misspent?
4. How do you distinguish between acting responsibly and
   being a meddler?
5. Is Raymond doing the right thing by reporting what he
   saw?

# The Problem:
## Civic Duty versus Being a Busybody

This is a story about our obligations in the public realm. Often there isn't much of a question about what we owe the government, although we may play around the edges. We pay our taxes—more or less on time. We report to jury duty when summoned—if we can't find a good excuse. We follow the law—except those that are simply so petty that we can ignore them or get away with breaking them. But this situation is different. Raymond's actions aren't about following rules as they apply to himself, but about what to do when others may not be fulfilling their obligations.

If Raymond decides to report the sleeping employees, he could be accused of being a busybody. It's easy to abide by the cliché, let sleeping dogs lie, so to speak. But here, there is more than meets the eye. One way to start thinking about the problem is to change the conditions just a little. Say Raymond owned his own business and saw two of his employees napping in the middle of the afternoon. He'd be a damn fool and a poor businessman if he ignored it. Maybe he'd talk to them privately, maybe he would put them on notice, or maybe he would even fire them. If he didn't do anything about lazy employees who worked for him, we would say that he is a bad manager and a worse owner.

## Everyone Is the Public

Public business isn't the same as private business, though. If I own something, then I am responsible for it. Everyone owns the government in a democratic society, at least in theory, so everyone is responsible in theory. Social psychologists know that it just doesn't work this way. Most of the time when everyone is responsible, no one acts responsibly. That's why, generally, private homes are taken care of better than public housing, and employees who have a stake in their work through some sort of ownership tend to be better motivated than people who simply work for a fixed salary.

This may be an accurate description of people's behavior, but a description doesn't tell us what we *ought* to do.

Whether Raymond should do something about workers who don't do what they are supposed to is, in one sense, a matter of fairness. Start from the premise that working conditions should be fair. This means, at the least, that people receive a decent wage for a job fairly done. Then assume that a person is, in fact, receiving a good salary and getting fair compensation for his labor. The other half of the work-fairness equation, then, is that a person who isn't working when he is supposed to is taking something that he isn't entitled to—namely, money without having earned it. Under such conditions, one ethical consideration is whether others have to work harder to make up for the work not done by the slackards. Another ethical issue is the breaking of an agreement by employees whose condition for employment is an understanding regarding the amount of work expected from them. Employees, in other words, have responsibilities to both their coworkers and their employer.

Occasionally I have reported rude or incompetent employees to their boss. As a customer I expect respectful and prompt service. Owners have a right to know why I, as a consumer, am upset. This gives them the chance to make changes if they so choose. With my complaint, I am trying to persuade the business to alter something I don't like. As a customer, I have a right to complain, although I may choose not to exercise it. I may think the situation is hopeless; I may feel uncomfortable with confrontation. But there is nothing wrong with complaining—provided there is some objective basis to the complaint.

I complain about those things that affect me. Something is done to me that I don't like or I don't get something that I think I deserve. I also take action when I think that social conditions are unjust, when I believe people are oppressed or threatened. So when I see the United Parcel Service truck parked near the tennis courts in the afternoon, I don't dial my local UPS office to tell them what I saw. To take such action would make me a busybody. On the other hand, if I have sat around all day waiting for a delivery and see the truck without a driver for hours on end, I wouldn't hesitate to lodge my complaint. Here the driver's indifference affects my life. I don't want to be captive in my house because the driver is slacking off.

Raymond's reaction is based upon a sense of being a good citizen. Reporting public employees who aren't doing their job is like turning off a running fire hydrant: both are wasting taxpayers'—and his—money. He has a civic duty to ensure to the best of his ability that the government runs efficiently.

## Assuming Too Much

Raymond doesn't stand in the same relation to these workers as an employer does to an employee, or as a customer to an owner. As an owner, he could penalize poor work; as a customer he could take his business elsewhere. Furthermore, he isn't directly hurt by their laziness. It isn't even certain what they *should* be doing.

It is here that Raymond has gone wrong. He takes action without first checking the facts. He assumes that the two in the truck cab are shirkers, but he is not certain. Perhaps they were done with the day's work and decided they would rather doze on the seat than go home to sleep. Or maybe they were early for their next job and needed to wait somewhere. Other possibilities, however unlikely, come to mind. The point is that Raymond really doesn't know what is going on. He has an interpretation of what he sees but he makes no effort to check out this interpretation with an informed source.

In addition, he doesn't know what the consequences are of his making the report. The possibilities range from the supervisors having a good laugh ("Imagine someone thinking that public employees should put in an honest day's work!") to the slackers being fired. Raymond's objective is to get them to do the work for which they are getting paid. But is he willing to risk them getting fired because of his indignation? Is their offense so grave that they ought to be deprived of their jobs?

A large problem with public ownership is that few people take responsibility for it. Raymond is an exception to the rule of indifference. He has a proprietary sense about government and its workers. He responds as though he employed them, which in a sense he does. But in his desire to act as a responsible citizen, he ignores the human relations dimension.

The best thing would be for him to go to the truck, talk to the workers, and ask if everything is all right.

"I've noticed that you have been here for a few hours. I just want to make sure you're okay," he could say to them.

Then if they told him to mind his own business, he might pursue it further. Either he could continue to talk to them (if he had the nerve) or report their rudeness, at least, to their supervisor.

But without first giving them a chance to explain themselves or putting them on warning, Raymond is placing them at an unfair disadvantage. It seems to me that the only reason he doesn't talk to them is that he doesn't have the courage to. This small example shows why the Greeks considered courage a necessary virtue, for without it the right thing often gets left undone.

# Obligations May Differ
# According to Gender and Place

This all seems pretty clear to me. But when I presented the situation to a class of mine at the university, some of the students pointed to something I hadn't considered. What if, they asked, it wasn't Raymond who saw the sleeping workers, but Raymonda? Wouldn't I judge the situation differently? It is true that a woman may feel that she is putting herself at risk by confronting two strange men. People aren't required to put themselves in harm's way for trivial reasons. It's a matter of proportion. This is another variation of the familiar adage "The punishment should fit the crime." Furthermore, in this instance, it seems that the problem can be handled in another way. So for Raymonda, the moral thing may also be the prudent one.

Another assumption of mine was pointed out by Confucian scholar Whalen Lai, who is the director of Religious Studies at the University of California at Davis. "In American society, a good reason to report on lazy municipal workers (higher morals aside) is that we pay our taxes and city workers are supposedly to be answerable to us. We do not pay them to be lazy. In imperial China, it would have been different. There law was imperial law and came down from above, so the last person you wanted to antagonize was the *yamen* runner. Whether he does his job or not is something he answers to his superior for. Not to you. He is the contact person between you and the state, so you don't want to ruffle his feathers, because if he wants to make trouble for you, there would be no end to your being harassed. The idea of government of the people, for the people, by the people is alien. And Chinese children were brought up with the fear of the policeman. All citizens, innocent or guilty, feared the policeman. He wasn't your servant; he was an extension of the mandarin and all the way back to the emperor. Even now, politicians point to the relative 'peace and quiet' of Chinatown as compared with, say, the black ghettos. But that is in part due to this thing about the Chinese running their own business (through their network of connections, not without its share of corruption) and on not 'making trouble' (alerting the authorities) that in traditional times usually only meant courting trouble for oneself."

Lai makes an important point and it is similar to the one made by my students. We have to take into account who is doing what under what circumstances; what is the likely outcome, and is the benefit worth the risk?

This vignette is a striking example of the need to understand the entire context of a situation. In other words, what is right hinges on the circumstances surrounding the incident. It is a good illustration of how ethics is often relative.

# Afterword

❧

I've never been good in math. Arithmetic has always given me a headache. I have trouble adding correctly, so it's no surprise that my wife takes care of our family finances. I can't balance a checkbook, so this is a good way to keep us out of trouble.

There is a great temptation to do something similar when it comes to difficult moral problems. I just want to turn them over to someone else.

"Just tell me what to do!" I want to say.

I can even find people who are happy to tell me, too. But I know that while this may relieve my immediate stress, it really is no solution at all. Ethics is a matter of choosing, and if someone makes our choices for us, we are no longer talking about ethics but something else entirely.

If you are concerned with moral behavior, if you want to improve your ethical IQ, then there's no getting around the necessity for making choices. And good choices require good judgment.

This is what this book has been about—helping you to develop the skill to make more comprehensive, complex, and nuanced judgments. And as with any skill, you become better and better with practice.

So now that you've come to the end, are you any more ethical than you were before you began? Well, maybe so. One way to check is to return to the questionnaire in chapter 3. Answer one more time. Now compare your answers to the ones you gave before. Has anything changed? If so, why have you changed your responses? What reasons do you now have for your choices?

It would be wonderful if life weren't filled with so many difficult ethical problems. But it is. Every day we must decide whether our actions harm or benefit others. It is an aspect of human nature to be part of the wider world. We have been blessed with the capacity to reason. So let's use it as best we can to help make life better for others and ourselves. One way to do this is to be as thoughtful as we can. I hope that by reading this book, by giving some consideration to ethical theory, and by giving much thought to the problems presented here, you will find delight in better being able to solve some of the ethical issues that confront you.

# Selected Bibliography

Cohen, Morris R. *The Faith of a Liberal.* Rutgers: Transaction Books, 1993.

Freeman, Derek. "Paradigms in Collision: Margaret Mead's Mistake and What It Has Done to Anthropology." *Skeptic*, vol. 5, no. 3, 1997, 66–73.

Gates, Henry L. Jr. "The End of Loyalty." *The New Yorker*, March 9, 1998.

Hacohen, Shmuel A. *Touching Heaven, Touching Earth: Hassidic Humor and Wit.* Tel Aviv: Sadan Publishing, 1976.

Hendin, Herbert. "Physician-Assisted Suicide: What Next?" *The Responsive Community*, vol. 7, no. 4, 1997, 21–34.

Hunt, Arnold D., Marie T. Crotty, and Robert B. Crotty. *Ethics of World Religions.* San Diego: Greenhaven Press, 1991.

Huntington, Anna Seaton. "The Shot Heard Round the Wrangle: Score One for the Record Book, but a Disservice to Her Game." *New York Times*, March 1, 1997.

Inbau, Fred E. (ed.). *Criminal Interrogation and Confessions, 4th Edition.* Gaithersburg: Aspen Publishers, 2001.

Lapham, Lewis H. *Waiting for the Barbarians.* New York: Verso, 1998.

Larmore, Charles E. *Patterns of Moral Complexity.* New York: Cambridge University Press, 1987.

Maimonides, Moses. *Guide for the Perplexed*. London: East and West Library, 1952.

"Progress Report on Alzheimer's Disease." Silver Spring, Md.: National Institute on Aging/National Institutes of Health, 1997.

Shields, David L. L., and Brenda Jo Light Bredemeir. *Character Development & Physical Activity*. Champaign, Ill.: Human Kinetics, 1995.

Shipler, David. *A Country of Strangers: Blacks and Whites in America*, New York: Alfred Knopf, 1997.

Worden, Leon. "Armageddon on Racial Preferences: An Interview with Ward Connerly." *The Signal*, www.the-signal.com/ editorial/ worden/.

# The Interviewees

West Point Military Academy graduate **Stephen Arata** has served in command positions in Germany, Panama, and Haiti. He is currently an assistant professor of history at West Point.

**Joan Beder,** who teaches social work at Yeshiva University, writes frequently about social work and medical ethics.

Now an owner of a children's clothing manufacturing company, **Laura Bernstein** worked for a decade as a magazine editor in California.

**Bill Brisotti,** pacifist and social justice activist, is a parish priest whose ministry is with the Hispanic community. He has been arrested several times for acts of civil disobedience and has spent much time in Central America working with peasant farmers.

**Joseph Chuman** is leader of the Ethical Culture Society of Bergen County, New Jersey. He teaches a graduate course on human rights at Columbia University and philosophy at Fairleigh Dickinson University.

Independent scholar and social critic **Barbara Ehrenreich** is the author of fifteen books, including *The End of Caring* and *A Progressive Social Agenda*.

Former president of the American Sociological Association, **Amitai Etzioni** is University Professor at George Washington University and is the founder of the communitarian movement. He has written extensively on ethics and responsibility.

**David Harmon,** director of the Counseling Center at St. John's University, is a member of the Human Rights Commission of Nassau County, New York.

**Sherry Hartwell** is a psychotherapist specializing in marriage, family, and children. She teaches the course Psychology of Women at Palomar Community College in San Diego.

Rabbi **Michael Katz** is the coauthor of *Swimming in the Sea of Talmud: Lessons for Everyday Living.*

Scholar of Confucian philosophy **Whalen Lai** is the director of Religious Studies at the University of California at Davis.

**Ellen McBride,** a lawyer who sits as a small-claims arbitrator, is the past president of the American Ethical Union.

**John S. Mbiti** is a theologian who has taught at universities in Africa and Europe. In 1998, he was professor of world religions at Princeton Theological Seminary; he presently lives in Kenya.

**Diana Nyad** is currently the senior correspondent for Fox Sports News and a columnist for National Public Radio's "Morning Edition." She holds the record for the longest swim in history—102.5 miles—which she set in 1979 by swimming from the island of Bimini to Florida. In 1986, she was inducted into the National Women's Sports Hall of Fame.

Disability case manager and rehabilitation counselor **Milagros Sanchez** founded a private vocational rehabilitation facility in Los Angeles and now works in Miami.

The author of the most popular book on ethics ever written, *Practical Ethics*, and the intellectual founder of the animal rights movement, **Peter Singer** teaches philosophy at Princeton University.

**Rick Seifert** was part of the Longview, Washington, *Daily News* team that won a 1981 Pulitzer Prize for its coverage of the Mount St. Helens eruption.

**David Sprintzen,** professor of philosophy and codirector the Institute for Sustainable Development at Long Island University, is the author of *Camus: A Critical Examination* and the founder of the Long Island Progressive Coalition.

**Carol Targum** is a psychotherapist specializing in families who have experienced trauma. She teaches social work at Widener University in Delaware.

Psychiatrist **Steven Targum,** the former medical director of Corzier Hospital, is a medical researcher on the causes of Alzheimer's disease.

**George Vecsey,** sports columnist for the *New York Times*, is the former religion editor for that newspaper. He is a recipient of an Amnesty International award for his book *Troublemaker,* with Harry Wu.

# INDEX